Companion
to
Global Praise 1 and *2* Songbooks

Worship Leader's Guide

Edited by
S T Kimbrough, Jr.

Published by the General Board of Global Ministries
GBGMusik
475 Riverside Drive
New York, NY 10115

ISBN 1-890569-93-3

Manufactured in the United States of America

Contents

Introduction

Global Praise 1 and *Global Praise 2* are the primary collections of global Christian song produced by the Global Praise Program of the General Board of Global Ministries. Neither of these songbooks could have come to realization without the diligent work of the Global Praise Working Group, a group of authors and composers from around the world which is convened annually by the Mission Evangelism office of the General Board of Global Ministries of The United Methodist Church. It should be noted that these songbooks are strongly ecumenical in content and may be used across a wide spectrum of worshiping Christian communities.

With songs from so many different regions, nations, cultures, and languages and with such diverse musical and rhythmic qualities, how are Christians of many lands to sing one another's songs? This book attempts to bring together as much background information as possible about each song and to address its theme, liturgical use, performance, and style. Where possible, there are indications of instrumentation. The presentations are not equal in length, as there is more information available about some songs than others.

The editor is deeply grateful to the members of the Global Praise Working Group for their untiring efforts in providing information about the songs included here: Tomas Boström, Melva W. Costen, the late Tom S. Colvin, Ludmila Garbuzova, Hartmut Handt, Per Harling, Marilyn M. Hofstra, I-to Loh, Mary K. Jackson, Ivor H. Jones, Jorge Lockward, Patrick Matsikenyiri, Simei Ferreira da Barros Monteiro, George Mulrain, David Pluess, Joyce Sohl, Pablo Sosa, Carlton R. Young. In addition, numerous authors and composers whose works are included in these two songbooks have responded with extremely helpful information about their own compositions, and, on occasion, those of others. A special word of thanks is extended to Jorge Lockward for technical and editorial assistance.

We sincerely hope that the material included in the *Companion* will help many to discover the songs which can be shared from diverse cultures, nations, and languages, and that they will strengthen and affirm one another in the journey with Christ and the church. As they are sung, the gospel of Jesus will be proclaimed in new, exciting, and effective ways; and the life, worship, and witness of Christians will be greatly enriched.

S T Kimbrough, Jr., Editor

Global Praise 1

1, Agios O Theos / Holy God

Author/Composer: Unknown
Background: This selection includes the Greek text of the Trisagion
(Thrice Holy), though the English is a free paraphrase—*ischyros*
meaning "strong" and *athanatos* meaning "immortal." This ancient
text became popular during the first Christian millennium and was
chanted in combination with psalm verses during elaborate
processions. The precise origin of the Trisagion is not known. It is
likely that it "was used only when the liturgy was preceded by a
procession of a penitential, intercessory character."[1] By the sixth
century, it was incorporated in almost all liturgies of the early church.

> The text continues in popular usage in Orthodox liturgies, though
the structure and style of its presentation have changed. In current
Orthodox worship, the Trisagion has been separated from the psalm
verses, yet it has retained a portion of its function as an introit hymn.

Theme: The hymn consists of two parts: (a) an affirmation or exclamation,
and (b) a prayer.
Liturgical use: In contemporary practice, worshipers recall the ancient
song of the angels: "Holy, holy, holy." As the Trisagion is sung, the
celebrant moves to the high place, or bishop's throne, in preparation
for the reading of the epistle and the gospel. It is excellent as an introit.
Performance and style: It is sung *a cappella*.

2, Aleluya

Author: Traditional text
Composer: Simei Monteiro, b. 1943, Brazil
Background: This song was composed to be sung as an *alleluia* in an
inculturated and very joyful way. In Latin America more and more one
can see among the "Base" communities what they used to call "the
celebration of the Word," when the Bible is brought into the church
and put on the altar or lectern. Thus the *aleluya* celebrates the Word.
"Base" communities are groups of faithful people—sometimes
ecumenical, sometimes only Roman Catholic—which gather to
celebrate their faith, God's presence, and the Word of God in their
midst, and to affirm the hope of God's reign being manifested among
them. Hence, it is sometimes a movement for justice and human rights,
but in the context of the people of God affirming God's reign.

9

Theme: Celebration and joy

Liturgical use: Psalm response. Easter, acclamation of the Word, and other places in the liturgy where an *alleluia* is appropriate.

Performance and style: It is essentially a congregational song. As a two-voice canon, it may be sung as follows: men and women, congregation and choir. The song is conceived in a *baião* rhythm: a dotted eighth + a sixteenth tied to a half note. If sung as a canon, attention must be paid to the faster notes (sixteenth notes) and the percussion beat. It could be danced in procession and/or around the altar. Tempo: quarter note = 120.

Instrumentation: Instruments that are appropriate for the *baião* rhythm (see explanation of #47 in *GP2*): accordion (or its sound on a synthesizer), floor tam (*zabumba*), triangle.

Teaching tips: Teach the melody first, then add rhythm and instruments. Use clapping only for rehearsal in order to capture the rhythm and to be able to dance it.

Reference: Look for sites on the Internet about: *baião*. See *GP2*, #47.

3, Alleluia

Composer: Wolfgang Amadeus Mozart, b. 1756, d. 1791, Austria

Background: This is an excerpt from Mozart's well known setting of the *alleluia* for soprano voice. In the 1970s, S T Kimbrough, Jr., heard the late Father William Travers, priest of the St. Thomas Moore Roman Catholic Church in Bonn, Germany, often use the two phrases included here in a call and response pattern at the appointed place for the *alleluia* in the liturgy. Father Travers would sing the first two *alleluias* and the congregation would respond with the final two *alleluias*.

Theme: It is an outburst of praise to God for the grace expressed in Jesus Christ.

Liturgical use: The *alleluia* usually occurs at an appointed place in the liturgy of the Eucharist, except during Lent.

Performance and style: It is used in a call-and-response style with a leader/cantor/choir singing the first two *alleluias* and the congregation responding with the last two *alleluias*. Tempo: quarter note = ca. 120.

4, Amen siakudumisa / Sing amen, we praise your name

Author/Composer: Unknown; arr. C. Molefe, South Africa, as taught by
George Mxadana; German trans., Dieter Trautwein, b. 1928, d. 2002,
Germany
Background: This song invokes praise and recognizes the presence of the
Lord.
Theme: The song stresses the gratitude of the congregation for the Word
that is to be delivered or has been proclaimed already.
Liturgical use: Christian year—general use; opening of worship, praise. It
is appropriate with movement, e.g., processional.
Performance and style: Maintain a lively tempo and sing with joy. This
energetic song originated among the Zulus and Xhosas, tribal peoples
of South Africa. Tempo: quarter note = ca. 98.
Teaching tips: Maintain a strong bass line. The leader sets the tone of the
song. Once set, the response should be lively and joyful.
Reference: It is recorded on *Africa Praise I* (CD 1-004, GBGMusik).

5, As your children, Lord

Author: Unknown
Composer: Unknown, African American melody; Russian trans., Ludmila
Garbuzova, b. 1948, Russia, and Irina Miagkova, Russia/USA.
Background: The music and English text appeared in the British
Methodist hymnal, *Hymns and Psalms* (1983). The tune is the well
known melody of "Kum bah yah," whose origin is considered to be
African American, though it has never been satisfactorily traced. The
Russian text originated at a meeting of The Russian Initiative of the
General Board of Global Ministries in 1995. S T Kimbrough, Jr., was
seated at a table with Ludmila Garbuzova and Irina Miagkova and
suggested that they make a Russian translation of this song, which he
was about to introduce. Irina Miagkova translated the meaning of the
text to Ludmila Garbuzova and the Russian text, which appears here,
was the result.
Theme: God's people are present to worship the Holy One. They come as
God's children.
Liturgical use: Christian unity, Holy Communion; opening of worship
Performance and style: Do not rush. When the leader has sung through
once, the congregation will follow thereafter without hesitation.

Simply line out the additional stanzas, each one of which is repeated three times within one cycle of a stanza. The Russian translation of the text is found in the Appendix at 5a. The Russian romanized transliteration is found at selection number 5. When using the Russian text with a non-Russian-speaking audience, use stanza 1, noting that the first line of each stanza is repeated three times in each stanza and only the final line after the third repetition is different. This greatly facilitates the learning process. Do not try to teach the Russian text all at one time. Be content with learning one or two stanzas well, and sing the rest of the song in English. As the text is gradually learned, you may find it possible to use all of the stanzas in Russian. Tempo: quarter note = ca. 72.

Reference: The song appears in the hymnal of the Russia United Methodist Church, *Mir Vam* (Peace be with you), published in 2002; henceforth cited as *MV* (2002). See *GP1* Appendix 5(a) for Russian text.

6, Ausgang und Eingang / Going and Coming

Author/Composer: Joachim Schwarz, b. 1930, d. 1998, Germany; Eng. trans., Dieter Trautwein, b. 1928, d. 2002, Germany

Background: The idea of the text is taken from Psalm 121:8 "The Lord will keep your going out and your coming in." The music describes the way from the beginning (upwards, opening bars of music) to the returning (downwards, last two bars of music).

Theme: Trust in God in every part of your way throughout life.

Liturgical use: The song is appropriate for the beginning and the ending of a meeting or worship service.

Performance and style: It may be sung rather slowly as a canon, with or without accompaniment. Conclude with a four-part chord at the end of every second bar.

Reference: This canon is published in the new *United Methodist Hymnal* in Germany, Austria, and Switzerland: *Gesangbuch der Evangelisch-methodistischen Kirche* (2002), Nr. 446; henceforth cited as *EM* (2002). Tempo: half note = 60.

7, Away with our fears

Author: Charles Wesley, b. 1707, d. 1788, Great Britain

Composer: Carlton R. Young, b. 1926, USA

Background: This hymn on the Incarnation by Charles Wesley was composed in a unique meter of three short lines of 5s, concluding with a long line of 11, (5 5 5.11) with the rhyme scheme AABB. It was first published in *Hymns for the Nativity of Our Lord (*1745). The tune was written for the composer's son Robert and included in *New Songs of Rejoicing* (Selah Publishing Co., 1994).

Theme: The Incarnation of God in Jesus Christ occasions the removal of fears among those who have confidence and trust in the redemptive love of God through the divine Son.

Liturgical use: It is appropriate for Advent and Christmastide.

Performance and style: The 1st and 5th stanzas may be sung by the whole group/congregation, and soloists may sing stanzas 2, 3, and 4; the group/congregation may repeat the last four words of each stanza as included in endings 1-4: "Jesus the child," "manger he lies," "holiness shine." Tempo: dotted quarter note = 48.

Reference: The song also appears in *MV* (2002).

8, God of Creation (Benediction)

Author/Composer: M. Thomas Thangaraj, b. 1941, India

Background: Dr. Thangaraj, the D. W. and Ruth Brooks Professor of World Christianity, Candler School of Theology, Emory University, is the author/composer. He is a native of India and composes here in an Indian style.

Theme: It is a prayer asking God the Trinity to send forth the people of God.

Liturgical use: It is appropriate at the close of any worship as a benediction and sending forth. It may be used at any time in the Christian year.

Performance and style: The men may sing the open fifth interval as a drone through the entire piece. They should stagger their breathing so that one has a continuous blanket of sound underneath the treble vocal line, which is to be sung by a soloist or by all female voices. Tempo: half note = ca. 60. The hymn is best conducted in 2/2 time.

Instrumentation: The drone tones C and G may be played on the organ or hummed by men, as noted above, throughout the piece. A finger cymbal may be struck on the first beat of every fourth measure. A pair of Indian drums (*tabla*) or conga drum accompaniment will add the

Indian flavor, though simple rhythms are intended.

Teaching tips: Have men hum the drones for four counts (two measures); then the leader or the choir sings up to the first amen. Thereafter the congregation may join in singing the second time. It may also be taught antiphonally, in four-measure phrases.

9, Bring many names

Author: Brian Wren, b. 1936, United Kingdom
Composer: Carlton R. Young, b. 1926, USA
Background and theme: This text about naming, addressing, and describing the Deity was significantly reworked by the author at the request of the Hymnal Revision Committee that produced *The United Methodist Hymnal*, 1989, but was rejected at the committee's final meeting because of the reference at 2:1: "Strong mother God, working night and day." While theologically apt for some, for others it was offensive and unacceptable. During the 1990s, several denominational hymnals have included the hymn, finding its language in concert with Genesis 5, that both male and female qualities originate in God. The Broadway-style tune is named WESTCHASE after the composer's former residence in Nashville, Tennessee.
Liturgical use: It is appropriate as a hymn of praise, for the opening of worship, and as a processional hymn.
Performance and style: Have the group/congregation sing stanzas 1 and 6, soloists or a small group stanzas 2-5, with the larger group singing the phrase beginning, "Hail and Hosanna." If the liturgy or context permits, faith stories about "strong mother God," "warm father God," "old aching God," and "young growing God," may be shared after singing each stanza or following stanza 6. Tempo: half note = 72.
Reference: It is recorded on *New Beginnings: the Music of Carlton R. Young* (CD 1-018, GBGMusik).

10, Brich mit den Hungrigen dein Brot / Break with the hungry your own bread

Author: Friedrich Karl Barth, Germany, b. 1938, Germany, theologian, author
Composer: Dieter Trautwein, b. 1928, d. 2002, Germany

Background: The song is written in an endless cycle, just as the task with which it deals is endless. The text, written by a German theologian/ author, consists of only five lines, which, like a chain, are formed differently in five stanzas each with only four lines. After line 5, you may start again from the beginning.

Theme: This song is about Christian acts of mercy: breaking bread with the hungry, sharing a kind word with the sorrowful, providing shelter for the homeless, etc.

Performance and style: One way to familiarize everyone with the impact of each line is to assign each line to respective groups, and when its line comes up in the song, each group sings its assigned text. Tempo: quarter note = 72.

Reference: There is a four-part choral setting published by the Christian Singers' Association (*Christlicher Sängerbund,* Germany).

11, Bèjé mouin, sé you Roua d'amou / The God of love my Shepherd is

Author: Unknown, based on Psalm 23; Eng. paraphrase, S T Kimbrough, Jr., b. 1936, USA

Composer: Unknown, transcribed by Carlton R. Young, as sung by Fede Jean-Pierre, b 1946, Haiti

Background and theme: This version of Psalm 23 is popular in the Caribbean republic of Haiti. It may be sung with a refrain. In #11, the refrain emphasizes that the Shepherd "will lead me where streams of living water flow and where the pleasant green pastures are to be found."

Performance and style: The arrangement is all the richer when played to the accompaniment of accordion, guitar, bass drum, congas, wood block, tambourine, and bass guitar. Tempo: quarter note = 60.

Liturgical use: This psalm is suitable for all occasions, including those in which people need to be reassured of God's providential care. When teaching this psalm to a congregation, it is preferable to have the people sing the refrain in Haitian Créole.

Reference: It is recorded on *Caribbean Praise* (CD 1-011, GBGMusik).

12, Christ Jesus my own Shepherd is

Author: Henry W. Baker, b. 1821, d. 1877, United Kingdom

Composer: Unknown; melody is sung to the same tune as Nr. 11.

Background and theme: This is also a paraphrase of Psalm 23. The refrain affirms that there is power in the name of Jesus. The psalm is relevant to the Haitian context in which, despite poverty and deprivation, people are convinced of God's care for and enduring goodness towards them.

Liturgical use: Same as for Nr. 11

Performance and style: Same as for Nr. 11

13 & 14, Bèjé mouin, sé you Roua d'amou / Adonai's my loving Shepherd

Text: Haitian hymn, as sung by Fede Jean-Pierre, b. 1946, Haiti; Eng. paraphrase, S T Kimbrough, Jr., b. 1936, USA; see Nr. 11.

15, Canção da caminhada / If walking is our vocation

Author/Composer: Simei Monteiro, b. 1943, Brazil; Eng. trans., Jaci Maraschin, alt., b. 1929, Brazil

Background: The song was conceived to express the theme of the Latin American Council of Churches: *Iglesia hacia una esperanza solidaria* (the church moving toward the hope of solidarity). There is a famous epic poem written by Luís de Camões entitled *Os Lusíadas,* which includes a verse that says: *navegar é preciso viver não é preciso.* The idea is that we need to sail if we want to live. This same idea is expressed in terms of walking (keep going); the need for perseverance in faith and then hope comes again. This is only possible when the community sustains the pilgrimage and believes that God is in its midst in hope and joyful solidarity.

Theme: This is a song of pilgrimage that may be understood in many ways: struggling for life, life in community (church), social concerns, solidarity in action.

Liturgical use: It is appropriate for a church's anniversary—when emphasizing or celebrating the church as a movement in faith and hope to express the concept of God's people continuing on the pilgrim road or faithfulness (perseverance) of believers; to express social concerns or for use on the occasion of inter-confessional and/or inter-faith celebrations.

Performance and style: The melody begins with a minor chord, and sometimes the key of C is not well perceived. The introduction must include chords that define the key of C. It is a *samba-canção*, which designates the rhythm of *bolero* in the Brazilian context. The melodic motif is repeated in an *expressivo* style. Movements could be improvised as a procession or along the rows of the church, expressing *the complicity of bodies in solidarity.* Explore the text and the idea of *singing on the way.* Ask for ideas as to how to perform the song with movements using the sequences of the melody. Tempo: quarter note = 85-110.

Instrumentation: Guitar, piano or keyboard, and some light percussion to keep the rhythm, e.g., bongo.

16, O-so-so, o-so-so / Come now, O Prince of Peace

Author/Composer: Geonyong Lee, b. 1947, Korea, Professor of Composition, Korean National Academy of Arts, Seoul; Eng. paraphrase, Marion Pope, American missionary

Background: The song was composed in 1988 while Professor Lee was attending a workshop at Bossey, Geneva, in which prayers for peace and reunification of North and South Korea were offered.

Theme: The primary themes are peace, freedom, unity, and reconciliation.

Liturgical use: It is appropriate as a response to prayers for peace and unity; each stanza may be sung individually as a response to each short prayer on related themes. It may be used at most any time of the Christian year and is particularly fitting for World Communion Sunday.

Performance and style: It may seem to some that there are missing notes in the alto part, at measure 3: G and Bb; on the second system: Eb, C, and C. The intentional dissonances and crossing of inner parts in the last two measures created by the composer should be respected. Tempo: quarter note = ca. 88.

Instrumentation: Keyboard, flute

Teaching tips: Triple rhythm is typical of Korean style. While the harmony is western, the melodic line is Asian in color and structure. Singing in unison, or with the choir humming the harmony, is also effective.

Reference: It is recorded on *Youth Praise: European Tour 1998* (CD 1-010, GBGMusik). It first appeared in *Sound the Bamboo* (1990). See *GP1* Appendix 16(a) for Korean text.

17, Child of joy and peace (Hunger Carol)

Author: Shirley Erena Murray, b. 1931, New Zealand

Composer: I-to Loh, b. 1936, Taiwan

Background: I-to Loh, ethnomusicologist and former president of
Tainan Theological College and Seminary, Taiwan, was deeply moved
and shocked by Murray's text: ". . . we deny you, by our greed we
crucify you on a Christmas tree, son of poverty." The composer
recalled his experience witnessing the severe poverty and suffering of
the Indonesian people, and he adapted a Balinese children's song that
seemed to convey the feeling of sadness, and utilized the gamelan
technique for the song's accompaniment. The main purpose was to
discourage people from using Christmas as an opportunity for wild
parties, and to encourage people to share food, care, and love with
starving babies around the world.

Theme: The song focuses on the meaning of Christmas: the nativity of
Christ, and the humanity of Christ have to do with hunger, poverty,
sharing of gifts, selflessness, Christmas tree, and crucifixion.

Liturgical use: The song fits any worship that centers around the meaning
of the Incarnation and salvation. It is perhaps best sung after the
sermon for reflection; it would also be meaningful before or after the
administration of the elements at Holy Communion. It may also have
the following liturgical uses: Advent, Christmastide, Love Feasts
(*agape* meals), etc.

Performance and instrumentation: In order to produce the effect of the
Javanese gamelan, a glockenspiel, chimes, or a harpsichord may be
used. Care must be taken to follow the phrasing of the figures—
imitation, anticipation, and decoration of the motifs—which are
important stylistic features of the *gamelan* technique. Tempo: quarter
note = ca. 72.

Teaching tips: Teach the choir or congregation to sing the scale in *pelog*
tuning: *mi fa sol ti do,* ascending and descending. Then one can sing
by rote: the congregation repeats phrase after phrase sung by the
leader.

Reference: A choral arrangement of the song with a recording was
published in *Church Music Workshop: Practical Tools for Effective
Music Ministry*, September-December, 1994, Abingdon Press.

18, No importa a la iglesia / No matter what church . . .

Text/Music: Cowboy folk ballad melody

Background: The melody for this popular Latin American worship chorus comes from the familar cowboy folk ballad "Red River Valley." This tune was originally associated with the song "In the Bright Mohawk Valley," a tune popular in New York. It is assumed that the tune was brought by missionaries from the United States to Latin America where they gave it a new text and added a refrain.

Theme: Christian unity, cooperation, mutual understanding. It fits appropriately with the Wesleyan affirmation, "If your heart is as my heart, then give me your hand."

Liturgical use: Ecumenical services, World Communion Sunday, peace and unity

Performance and style: This song should be performed in an upbeat tempo: quarter note = 100-120. It is particularily suited to the use of movement in worship. One of many possibilities is to ask people to shake hands during the refrain of the song.

Instrumentation: Guitar, bass guitar, keyboards, and percussion (especially tambourine) may be used. The song is normally interpreted in a polka style.

Teaching tips: The refrain (measures 17-32) may be taught in Spanish, given the repetition of its short and simple text. It is advisable to wait until the song is well learned before engaging the congregation in movement, such as shaking hands with one's neighbor during the refrain. Once the refrain has been memorized, it may be repeated *ad libitum* during the movements.

19, Dawk'yahee ahdawtsahee

Text/Music: Unknown, Kiowa Prayer Song

Background: Historically tribal elders taught children music, the meaning of the words, and how and when to sing them. When the children became elders, they too passed these cultural traditions on to their children. That is how songs were passed from generation to generation. This prayer song was first published in written form with western musical notation in Marilyn Hofstra's collection of Native

American Christian song: *Voices—Native American Hymns and Worship Resources.*

Theme: Prayer and worship

Liturgical use: Opening of worship and call to prayer

Performance and style: Historically, Native American hymns were sung without instruments. With each musical and oral repetition, the song should be easier to sing.

Follow these steps to learn the song:

1. Listen to and sing the melodic line until it becomes familiar.
2. Read and repeat the words until you become comfortable speaking them.
3. As you speak the words over and over, you will recall their meaning.

Reference: Voices—Native American Hymns and Worship Resources (Nashville: Discipleship Resources, 1992)

20, Dong tian yi wang / Winter has passed

Author: Wang Weifan, b. 1927, China; Eng. trans., Ewing W. Carroll, Jr., b. 1937, USA

Composer: Shengben Lin, b. 1927, China; arranger for second setting: Pen-li Chen, pen name for I-to Loh

Background: The three stanzas of "Winter is Past" were written in 1957 by the Christian, Wang Weifan. After graduating from Nanjing Theological Seminary in the 1950s, he worked for a local church until 1958, the year he wrote these stanzas. However, he did not write the chorus at this time. He was criticized during the Anti-Rightist campaign in 1958 and again during the so-called Cultural Revolution era [1966-76]. For most of the next twenty years, he was separated from his theological work, his home, and family, laboring in the countryside along with the rural peasant farmers.

In the early 1980s, Wang returned to Nanjing Union Seminary, where he now teaches, and found three stanzas of this poem among his papers there. He had not seen them since he had written them, twenty-five years before. In 1982, Wang Weifan was finally able to write the chorus for the stanzas which express longing for the assurance of a faithful God. The wistful longing for the Lover of lovers turns to joyous confidence in the chorus: "Jesus my Lord, my love, my all; / body and soul forever yours."

Theme: Devotion, trust, union with Christ, discipleship

Liturgical use: Use stanza 1 as a call to worship, and the refrain as a response or as a call to discipleship after the sermon. Stanza 3 may be used as a response for commitment and discipleship. It is also a metaphor for the relationship between the Bride (the church) and the Bridegroom (Christ). While the song may be used generally throughout the Christian year, it is appropriate for Easter.

Performance and style: The five-tone scale without a half step (*do re mi sol la*) and the traditional western four-part harmony are favorite styles of Chinese Christians. The alternative setting, however, uses imitative passages in the lower voice to symbolize following the footsteps of Jesus. It may be more interesting to use this setting for accompanying the third stanza. Compound triple rhythm is not typical of Chinese rhythm, so it would not be appropriate to emphasize too much the feeling of a dance rhythm. Tempo: eighth note = ca. 96.

Teaching tips: Try singing the five tone scale: *do re mi sol la.* For the second setting, a flute of any type may play the main melody, and a cello or stringed instrument for the accompaniment would be in keeping with Chinese style.

References: It is recorded by the Methodist Music School Choristers of Singapore on *Faith•Hope•Love* (CD 1-013 GBGMusik). A choral version is available in the *GP Choral Series* (CS 1008). See *GP1* Appendix 20(a) for Chinese (Mandarin) text.

21, 'Eiki ko e 'ofa 'a 'au / O hidden depth of love divine

Author: Johann Andreas Rothe, b. 1688, d. 1758, Germany; Eng. trans. from German by John Wesley, b. 1703, d. 1791. The Tongan translator is unknown; Eng. paraphrase, S T Kimbrough, Jr.

Composer: Unknown

Background: The translation from English into the Tongan language was dedicated to the work of the missionary, the Rev. Dr. Moulton, perhaps the translator. The composer of the tune is not known, but it is believed to have been composed by one of the early Methodist missionaries. Another tune has been composed by Alipate Tupouniua.

Theme: The three stanzas of John Wesley's translation of the Rothe hymn which were translated into Tongan are as follows:

21

O love, thou bottomless abyss,
    My sins are swallowed up in thee!
Covered in my unrighteousness,
    Nor spot of guilt remains in me.
While Jesus' blood through earth and skies
Mercy, free, boundless mercy! cries.

Though waves and storms go o'er my head,
    Though strength, and health, and friends be gone,
Though joys be withered all and dead,
    Though every comfort be withdrawn,
On this my steadfast soul relies—
Father, thy mercy never dies!

Fixed on this ground will I remain,
    Though my heart fail and flesh decay;
This anchor shall my soul sustain,
    When earth's foundations melt away:
Mercy's full power I then shall prove,
Loved with an everlasting love.

Liturgical use: Services of healing and reconciliation

Performance and style: The hymn is written in a gospel-song style
    and is effective when sung in unison or in four parts with
    keyboard accompaniment.

22, Kuo fekau 'a Sisu / To his followers Jesus spoke

Author/Composer: Unknown; Eng. paraphrase, S T Kimbrough, Jr., b.
    1936, USA, based on a translation by T. T. M. Puloka, Tonga

Background: This version of the hymn is excerpted from hymn 114
    in *Ko e Tohi Himi 'A e Stast Uesiltana Tau'aataina 'O Tonga* (The
    Hymnal of the Free Wesleyan Church of Tonga).

Theme: The hymn is based on the command of Jesus in Luke 21:36,
    "Watch therefore, and pray always, that you may be accounted worthy
    to escape all these things that shall come to pass, and to stand before
    the Son of man," and on Jesus' affirmation in Luke 18:1 that everyone
    ought "always to pray and not to faint." These words of Jesus also
    resonate in the Apostle Paul's admonition to the church at
    Thessalonica, "Pray without ceasing" (1 Thessalonians 5:17).

Liturgical use: Call to prayer

Performance and style: The hymn should be sung energetically but prayerfully and in parts, which signify the harmony that unifies all in prayer. The echoing bass and tenor lines serve to punctuate or underscore the confidence that God will hear prayer and respond to human need.

Instrumentation: Keyboard or brass instruments would be appropriate, but the hymn may also be sung *a cappella.*

23, Shalom chaverim / Peace be with you

Text/Music: Traditional Hebrew words and melody

Background: Shalom is the Hebrew word meaning "peace, well-being, wholeness." It is used in Hebrew as a word of greeting and of departure.

Liturgical use: Passing of the peace, benediction, and sending forth

Performance and style: Sing *a cappella* as a canon or round. Note the entrance numbers for three groups (1, 2, 3). A guide to pronunciation of the Hebrew is found at the bottom of the page in the *Global Praise 1* songbook. Tempo: quarter note = 96-100.

Reference: It is recorded on *Global Praise 1* (CD 1-003, GBGMusik).

24, The thirsty deer longs for the stream (Psalm 42)

Author: George Mulrain, b. 1946

Composer: Unknown

Background: The music is well known as a chorus sung in revivalist circles in the Eastern Caribbean.

Theme: This paraphrase to Psalm 42 is considered theologically relevant to the Caribbean. For one thing, it evokes the image of a people who constantly yearn for the presence of God. It emphasizes that Caribbean people are rarely troubled by difficult situations in which they might find themselves. Whether they face hurricanes or volcanoes, they still say "no problem"—a popular expression which signals their deep-rooted faith in God. Within the region, there is the conviction that God can always be trusted. Worthy of trust in the past and in the present, God can be relied upon fully in the future. In the final analysis, whatever the difficulty one might face, all will work out well.

Liturgical use: It may be sung as the appointed lectionary psalm, or used as a choral introit.

Performance and style: The song is written and sung in a calypso style, very characteristic of the Caribbean region. It should be sung energetically and with lively engagement. One need not stand still! Tempo: quarter note = ca. 120.

Instrumentation: Guitar, bass guitar, congas, tambourine, scraper (grater), saxophone (optional)

Teaching tips: It is advisable to teach the refrain first.

Reference: It is recorded on *Global Praise 1* (CD 1-003, GBGMusik), and on *Caribbean Praise* (CD 1-001, GBGMusik).

25, För livets skull / For sake of life

Author/Composer: Per Harling, b. 1948, Sweden; harm., Carlton R. Young, b. 1926, USA

Background: This is a theme song written for a large ecumenical meeting in Sweden during the summer of 1992. The theme for the meeting, "For sake of life," addressed the issues of justice, peace, and the integrity of creation, which by that time was a program of the World Council of Churches.

Theme: This is a song of hope, in which stanzas 1-3 focus on the different aspects of justice and peace work, as well as the need to care for the integrity of creation in order to share the "bread from common soil"—"for sake of life." In the last stanza, the Incarnation and reconciliation in Jesus Christ are addressed as being the starting point and the goal of the work to fulfill the Kingdom of God—"for sake of life." The song has become very popular in Sweden and is now one of the numbers in the official supplement to the hymnal of the Church of Sweden, *Psalmer i 90-talet* (1994).

Liturgical use: It may be used as a hymn/song in any worship service stressing the issues of justice, peace, and the integrity of creation.

Performance and style: The song has the flavor of a Swedish, folkloric style. Swedish folk music is mostly set in minor, as is much folk music. This song is also sung in a Spanish translation in many parts of Latin America. In Argentina it has been turned into a *tango!* Try to sing the song in different styles and find out if, and how, the style may affect the understanding of the song, both text and music. Tempo: eighth note = ca. 110.

Reference: The song is published in *EM* (2002).

26, Glauben heisst Christus / Trusting in Jesus

Author: Hartmut Handt, b. 1940, Germany
Composer: Paul Ernst Ruppel, b. 1913, Germany; (second musical setting at the bottom of the page) Alice Knotts, b. 1944, USA
Background: The text was inspired by the World Council of Churches Assembly in Nairobi, Kenya in 1975, reflecting on the theme "Jesus Christ frees and unites," and it reminds one of the affirmation of Nairobi: "The name of Jesus must be spoken." Handt is a pastor of The United Methodist Church in Germany and has written and translated many texts. Ruppel is a German church musician. Knotts is a pastor of The United Methodist Church.
Theme: An essential way of confessing Christian faith is doing faith, i.e., acting it out in one's life.
Liturgical use: The last two bars of each stanza may be used as a kind of antiphon or response during a prayer of intercession.
Performance and style: It may also be sung without instruments. Tempo for the Ruppel setting: quarter note = 96; tempo for the Knotts setting: dotted half note = 48.
Teaching tips: When teaching the tune, start with the last two bars, then go back to the beginning.
Reference: Three- and four-part vocal scores for choirs are published by the Christian Singers' Association (*Christlicher Sängerbund,* Germany), but only with the German text. The song appears in *EM* (2002).

27, Gloria, gloria, gloria

Words: Luke 2:14
Composer: Pablo Sosa, b. 1933, Argentina
Background: The children had everything ready for the Christmas pageant: the shepherds, the wise men, and of course, Jesus, Mary, and Joseph; even the angels. But (last minute problems!) whoever was supposed to teach the angels to sing their song had not done so. And who can imagine a choir of angels entering silently while someone reads "Glory be to God on high"?

So Pablo Sosa made up a very, very easy melody to sing, and before the play started he took a few minutes to teach it to the whole congregation. So that when the angels finally came in, wrapped in their clean, white linen, everyone sang for them:

> "Glory be to God on high,
> and on earth peace to the people
> in whom God is well pleased." (Luke 2:14)

Theme: The theme is twofold: the universality of God's love, and peace on earth as the consequence of God's praise. Through the Incarnation, all learn from God to proclaim the message of love and peace.

Liturgical use: Advent and Christmas, and after the declaration of forgiveness of sins.

Performance and style:

1. Sing the first phrase and *immediately,* without any comments or interruption of the rhythm, repeat it with the people while you conduct it. If possible (it's not difficult), do not beat time but show the height and length of the sounds in the air with your hands. It will help people to "see" the melody and remember it. Since this is a rather fast song, the movements will have to be very dynamic.
2. The song is easy to memorize. Have everyone put the book down as soon as possible.
3. Teach each phrase as you did the first.
4. Bring in the instruments to show the rhythm as they play on the first chord of the song (F).
5. Sing in a call-and-response pattern. You may alternate with men and women singing the melody. Always: *you sing, they repeat.*
6. Put both parts together. Several times sing *only the notes of the three "Glorias,"* slowly and vigorously. Then try singing the two complete phrases at normal speed.
7. If possible, add a third part: tenors. Teach it as you did the other two.
8. Put all the parts together. Try the *"Glorias"* again *slowly in three* Enjoy the sound! Tell everyone to listen to one another. Then try the entire song at normal speed.
9. Teach them to clap the 6/8 rhythm. They should clap only at the instrumental sections (introduction, interlude), not while they are singing. Try the whole song a couple of times, adding the clapping.
10. The tempo should be lively. This is a *cueca,* a song-dance, a folk style of the Andean region: Bolivia, Chile, Argentina. It should be *forte* but not *fortissimo.* Watch for the fading away at the very end, when "the angels fly away. . ." Tempo: eighth note = 80-84.

Rhythm: Note the superimposition of 6/8 and 3/4, and the *hemiola* at the end of the last phrase.

Instrumentation: Guitar, (harp) piano, light percussion. Encourage the use of the piano accompaniment in the *GP1* Appendix (27a).

Reference: It is recorded on *Global Praise 1,* (CD 1-001, GBGMusik); on the CD *Éste es el Día: Canciones de Pablo Sosa,* a product of ISEDET (Buenos Aires, Argentina); in German on the CD *Du bist der Atem meiner Lieder* (Anker Musik, Stuttgart, Germany). It is included in *EM* (2002). See *GP1* Appendix for alternate harmonization and piano accompaniment.

28, Gloria a Dios / Glory to God

Text/Music: Traditional Peruvian folk song

Background: This piece has great historical significance because of its association with the *Lima Liturgy 1982,* prepared by the World Council of Churches in consultation with the Roman Catholic Church. The song uses a traditional Peruvian melody as its tune. This particular tune is written in the *carnavalito* style, a pre-Columbian Andean dance rhythm. The text is based on a traditional liturgical text from the Gospel according to Luke 2:14 ("The Angel's Song").

Theme: This is a song of praise to the triune God.

Liturgical use: Although its intended use is for the *gloria* and *laudamus* of the Eucharistic celebration, this song can be used at any moment in worship that calls for doxology, celebration, and exaltation of the Trinity; for example, as:
- a response to the reading of the Gospel
- the doxology after the offertory
- an expression of praise and thanksgiving after particularly good news during announcements.

Performance and style: The inner rhythm of this song is so strong that it can be sung *a cappella* or accompanied with percussion instruments only. In case other instruments are desired, guitar and keyboards may be used.

The three *alleluias* that end the piece should be sung at increasing dynamic levels from *piano* to *forte.* Tempo: quarter note = 70.

Teaching tips: This song lends itself to many varieties of antiphonal use: (a) a leader answered by the congregation in a call and response style, (b) antiphonal choirs or sections of the congregation respond to one another in different languages. The antiphonal nature of this song makes it very easy to teach in the original Spanish.

29, Help us, Lord, to be peace-makers

Author: Thomas Stevenson Colvin, b. 1925, d. 2000, Scotland
Composer: John Stainer, b. 1840, d. 1901, Great Britain
Background: Tom Colvin, theologian, collector, translator, and publisher
   of African songs, was a missionary in Africa for thirty years. There he
   listened carefully to the sounds, needs, and expressions of the people
   he served. He had a special gift for writing song texts which bring
   together many of these elements from African cultures. One thing
   of which he was keenly aware was the desire of the people of Africa
   for peace, a desire which he articulated eloquently in this song text.
   The tune is not African, rather quite British, being from John Stainer,
   well-known British church musician/composer.
Theme: Those trusting in Jesus make peace. Peacemakers are very
   precious in God's sight and are themselves really free, even when they
   are imprisoned. This is truly a song of Christian social holiness.
Liturgical use: The song is fitting for World Communion Sunday,
   ecumenical services of worship, days of national observance, and
   Holy Communion.
Performance and style: It may be accompanied by a keyboard, piano,
   organ, guitar, or sung *a cappella* in SATB harmony. Tempo: quarter
   note = 88-96.
Reference: The song appears with a different tune in *EM* (2002).

30, God of every nation / Bozhe nash spaseetyel

Author/Composer: Anonymous
Background: S T Kimbrough, Jr., first discovered this hymn in the
   Russian hymnbook, *Songs of Zion,* published in 1925 in Harbin
   (Manchuria), China, by the Methodist Episcopal Church, South, for its
   Russian congregations there. The hymnbook included many songs
   from worldwide Christendom but also a considerable number of
   indigenous Russian hymns. This hymn was the last in the hymnbook.
Theme: It is a plea that God will save Russia. While the original Russian-
   language refrain specifically says, "Save Russia," an alternate rendering, "Our nation's praying," has also been included so that people of
   all nations may offer this prayer for their own nation.
Liturgical use: World Communion Sunday, ecumenical services, Thanksgiving, and Harvest Festival

Performance and style: The hymn is written in a forthright style of Russian Protestant hymns, such as those by Ivan S. Prochanov (see *GP2,* #104). The tune is similar to that of many central European melodies from the eighteenth and nineteenth centuries, though perhaps more extended. One could perform it in the following sequence: stanza 1 plus refrain, stanzas 2 and 3 plus refrain. The refrain would be omitted between stanzas 2 and 3 in this sequence. Tempo: half note = 68-72.

Reference: It appears in *Russian Praise* and on its companion recording (CD 1-006, GBGMusik), and in *MV* (2002). See *GP1* Appendix for Russian (Cyrillic) text and romanized transliteration.

31, Halle, halleluja

Text/Music: Traditional Caribbean song; stanzas:
text and arr., George Mulrain, b. 1946, Trinidad and Tobago;
musical arr., Carlton R. Young

Background and theme: The refrain of this song is extremely popular and known throughout the Caribbean region. For the stanzas which have been added, George Mulrain has appropriated lines from the hymn, "Rock of Ages cleft for me." When he examined the text, he was not sure that the words "I am the rock of ages cleft for me" or "I am the let me hide myself in thee" made for ready comprehension. Therefore he decided not only to add verses to what was already in existence, but to reinterpret what was actually there. Hence, there is an emphasis upon God, the great I AM, the one who revealed the divine self to Moses. The I AM also was made to point directly to Jesus. According to the Gospel of John, there are seven "I am" sayings attributed to Jesus, including "I am the Bread of Life, . . . the One True Vine, . . . the Resurrection, . . . the Way, the Truth, and the Life." The theological emphasis of the song is that Jesus Christ is everything.

Performance and style: Begin by teaching the chorus, which people will pick up very quickly. The song must be sung energetically and with a driving rhythm. At the outset, have a choir or soloist sing the stanzas and have the congregation join the singing at the chorus. When the congregation has heard the song once or twice with the stanzas, it will sing them readily. Tempo: quarter note = 76-96.

Liturgical use: It is appropriate as a song to introduce the ministry of the Word, or to end worship on a celebrative note. It is very fitting for the

Festival of Christ the King.

Instrumentation: Suggested accompaniment: steel pans, piano, guitar, bass guitar, flute/piccolo, drum set, congas, strings (optional).

Reference: It is recorded on *Caribbean Praise* (CD 1-011, GBGMusik).

32, Heleluyan / Hallelujah

Author/Composer: Traditional Muscogee (Creek) Native American song

Background: Historically, tribal elders taught children the meaning of the music and words, and how and when to sing them. When the children became elders, they too passed these cultural traditions on to their children. In this way, songs were passed from generation to generation.

Theme: Christian people sing "Heleluyan/Hallelujah" because there are Christians, ministers, elders, and young people in heaven. The song affirms our interrelationships and our common bond with God, the Great Spirit and Creator of all.

Liturgical use: Opening of worship; appropriate for praise and thanks-giving

Performance and style: Follow these steps to learn these two songs:
1. Listen to and sing the melodic line until it becomes familiar.
2. Read and repeat the words until everyone is comfortable speaking them.
3. As the words are repeated over and over, their meaning will be recalled. Historically, Native American hymns were sung without instruments. Each musical and oral repetition will come more easily every time one repeats the words.

Reference: It is recorded on *Make Plain the Vision: Songs of Women* (CD 1-007, GBGMusik, section: "Voices of Vision"). See the collection, *Voices—Native American Hymns and Worship Resources* (Nashville: Discipleship Resources, 1992).

33, Helig, helig, helig / Holy, holy, holy

Text: Liturgical text of the *sanctus*

Composer: Lars Åberg, b. 1948, Sweden; Eng. trans., S T Kimbrough, b. 1936, USA

Background: The main Lutheran church in Sweden, the Church of Sweden, has deep liturgical roots in pre-Reformation times. Thus, most official liturgical melodies still are sung in a Gregorian style. Officially, one may use five different settings for the *sanctus* and *benedictus*. One of them (the newest one) is from 1544. All the others are from the tenth to the twelfth centuries. In the beginning of the 1990s one of the delegates in the Church of Sweden Synod asked for new, modern settings for the old, liturgical texts. This composition of Lars Åberg was one of the settings that resulted from the efforts to find new compositions for the traditional liturgical music of the Church of Sweden. Åberg is a well-known cathedral organist in Sweden who has a broad knowledge of a wide range of musical styles. He is a diploma organist, trained in Sweden as well as in Holland and other countries in Europe. At the same time, he is known for his very simple youth songs.

Liturgical use: The appropriate use of this piece is at the appointed place of the *sanctus* and *benedictus* in a service of Holy Communion. However, it may also be used as an opening song of praise and processional.

Performance and style: This song was composed intentionally in a Swedish folk-music style, more specifically in a march style, which often is used by folk fiddlers at weddings. It is actually good to walk while singing this *sanctus*. Thus it becomes a pilgrim song, a song for pilgrims on the move. Tempo: half note = 56.

Teaching tips: Play it once through (perhaps with fiddlers), sing it standing, and once more while moving!

Reference: The song is also published in *EM* (2002).

34, I am your mother (Earth Prayer)

Author: Shirley Erena Murray, b. 1931, New Zealand

Composer: Per Harling, b. 1948, Sweden; harm., Carlton R. Young, b. 1926, USA

Background: Shirley Erena Murray says about this hymn: "Living in New Zealand, with its 'green' culture and Maori creation stories, I feel strongly about the 'theology of the earth.' This is written in the first person to compel attention!"

Theme: In most cultures around the world, the earth is seen as a mother, receiving the resources for life—the seeds, the rain, and the sunshine —and giving life back to the world in the germination and growing of the seeds, in the streaming of the lifegiving waters, and in the process of photosynthesis, providing oxygen for our breathing. Now mother earth is threatened more than ever, so we need to listen to her own groaning. This is her groaning prayer, not to God above but to us, her dependent children.

Liturgical use: Whenever ecological, environmental issues are emphasized, this is the hymn to sing. It is especially appropriate for Thanksgiving and Harvest Festivals.

Performance and style: The music is written in a slow tempo, like a lullaby: picture a mother cradling her children in her warm and loving arms. Maybe a woman could be asked to sing the first stanza, when the song is being taught, and then let the people join in the rest of the song. The accompaniment should be simple and graceful. Tempo: quarter note = 106.

Reference: Recorded on *Make Plain the Vision: Songs of Women* (CD 1-007, GBGMusik).

35, Jag tror på en Gud / I believe in a God, one only

Author/Composer: Tomas Boström, b. 1953, Sweden; Eng. trans., Per Harling, b. 1948; harm., Carlton R. Young, b. 1926, USA

Background: This *Credo* was first included in confirmation materials, which used songs as teaching aids to learning and remembering essential beliefs of the Christian faith.

Theme: Central ideas of the Apostle's Creed are the focus of the text. This is a very typical Boström song that emphasizes the faith or belief that God's love and realm are in our hearts and that faith grows from within. Here we meet the Creator, the Love, the spiritual Mystery, and from our hearts God will lead us out to meet the world.

Liturgical use: It may be used at the place in the liturgy for the recitation of the creed, either the Apostles' Creed or Nicene Creed. It may also be used as a general hymn throughout the year.

Performance and style: You may sing this song very gently, if you wish, or with a stronger emphasis. This depends on the situation in which it is used. Guitar and keyboard are appropriate. Tempo: quarter note = 70.

Reference: It is recorded on *Global Praise 1* (CD 1-003, GBGMusik) and on *Du bist der Atem meiner Lieder* (Anker Musik, Germany). It appears also in *EM* (2002).

36, Jesu tawa pano / Jesus, we are here

Author/Composer: Patrick Matsikenyiri, b. 1937, Zimbabwe
Background and theme: The song draws attention to God the Son. This
is similar to what happens in an African village at the chief's court.
Before the people report to the chief that they have at last assembled in
accordance with his request, they gather and begin to talk, even joking
with the chief. If they do not respond in this way, he will not receive
them. The elder of the team will then summon the rest of the group to
come to order. The leader then says to the chief, "May we bring our
hands together to you?" (The literal meaning is: "May we clap our
hands to honor you, sir?") The chief's counselor will then pass the
word to the chief, who will in turn say, "Go ahead, my people."

   The counselor will then lead the audience in rhythmic clapping,
and when the chief greets the people, the meeting is officially in
session. "Jesus, we are here" serves as a signal that they are ready to
worship God.

   In the chapel service at Africa University (Old Mutare, Zimbabwe),
there is a tradition of singing as people gather, and at an appropriate
time they often sing "Jesus, we are here," signaling to everyone present that it is time to begin worshiping as per the order of service.
In a similar way, congregations receive a signal from the organist that
it is time to stand and sing the doxology at the presentation of the
offering.

   In this song, one addresses and beckons God to hear one's prayers
and petitions. One humbles oneself before the Lord and awaits the
divine command, advice, and blessing.
Liturgical use: It is effective as a call to worship. One might use it to
break in during the sermon to energize people, as an awakening
response to a sermon, or to invite people to prayer after the sermon.
Performance and style: Keep a steady beat, with the leader adding
innovations and/or embellishments. As one addresses the persons of
the Trinity, one should anticipate their visitation. Tempo: quarter note
= 72-88.
Teaching tips: Begin with pronunciation of *tawa pano muzita renyu.* The
rhythm of this line is tricky but easy to get, if done correctly at the
beginning and before people succumb to their fears of another
language. A keyboard may be used to get people going, but it may

gradually fade away until the people are absorbed in the song without the keyboard. But the drum and the *hosho* (shaker) should take the keyboard's place. The whole song should conform to the mood of the service. It may also be used to enliven and motivate the congregation.

Reference: It is recorded by Africa University Choir on *Africa Praise 1,* (CD1-004, GBGMusik). A choral arrangement is available in the songbook *Africa Praise 1,* and in the *GP Choral Series, African Medley 2* (CS 1003), both available from GBGMusik. It appears also in *MV* (2002). The song is published in *EM* (2002).

37, Kadosh, we sing unto the Lord

Author/Composer: S T Kimbrough, Jr., b. 1936, USA

Background and theme: The author/composer has used some key words of the Hebrew Bible in a song of praise. *Kadosh* means "holy," *kabod* means "glory," and *gadol* means "great." Hence, when we utter these words in song, we link our voices with the cloud of witnesses back to the earliest period of the Hebrew peoples as they proclaimed, "God, you are holy; you are glory; you are great."

Liturgical use: The stanzas are intended for the liturgical punctuation of God's holiness, glory, and greatness at times of prayer, intercession, and praise.

Performance and style: Ask a cantor, soloist, or someone who sings well to sing the song through. That will usually be sufficient to establish the melody, which is quite simple. Then sing prayerfully and spiritually. Tempo: quarter note = 88.

Reference: An expanded keyboard accompaniment is available in the Appendix of the *GP1* songbook at 37(a). The song also appears in *MV* (2002).

38, Magnificat

Text: Luke 1:46

Composer: Jacques Berthier, b. 1923, d. 1994, France

Background: This is a setting of the opening statement of "Mary's Song" (Luke 1:46) by French composer Jacques Berthier for the Taizé community. See *GP2* #127 for more information on the author. Taizé is a Christian community in France which, since the end of World War 2, has focused on spirituality and worship. Jacques Berthier was one of its primary creators of short forms of liturgical songs, which have become popular throughout the world.

Theme: Praise to God for the promise of the Incarnation

Liturgical use: Use at any time in worship that calls for an expression of heartfelt praise. It is appropriate for Advent and Evening Prayer.

Performance and style: A tempo of half note = 54 is recommended. This piece should be sung in a flowing, uninterrupted manner with clear phrases articulated every two measures. Make sure that there is no delay from the end of a phrase to the beginning of the next. As a canon, this piece may be performed *a cappella.* If some instrumental support is desired, a minimal chordal accompaniment by organ, piano, or guitar may be provided using the following chord progression throughout: G C / D7 G.

The second canon (38a) is supplemental to the main canon and should be added by the choir or soloists once the first canon is well established.

Teaching tips: It is of utmost importance to be absolutely sure that the congregation knows and is comfortable with the melody before attempting to sing it in canonic form. Pre-assigning instrumentalists or singers to support the different parts of the canon may be very helpful.

References: The canon is published in *EM* (2002). Further choral and instrumental parts for this song may be found in:
> *Music from Taizé,* Vol. 1, published by GIA Publications, Inc., 7404 So. Mason Ave., Chicago, IL 60638; tel. 800 442-1358.

39, Komm, Herr, segne uns / Bless and keep us, Lord

Author/Composer: Dieter Trautwein, b. 1928, d. 2002, Germany

Background and theme: This song is a prayer for God's blessings with a special emphasis on the fact that God's blessings unite us and make us responsible for human fellowship. The song is well known in ecumenical circles.

Liturgical use: It is appropriate at the end of worship or a meeting. One or more stanzas might be used as a benediction or all stanzas sung as a concluding song or hymn.

Performance and style: The song may be sung *a cappella* or with different instruments. Tempo: half note = 64.

Reference: There is a four-part choral arrangement published by the Christian Singers' Association (*Christlicher Sängerbund,* Germany).

The song also appears in *EM* (2002).

40, Star–Child

Author: Shirley Erena Murray, b. 1931, New Zealand

Composer: Carlton R. Young, b. 1926, USA

Background: The composer set the text within a few hours of receiving it via the author's annual Christmas letter. It was first sung at the baptism of Lena Leibrook Wilson and Kirby Michael Wilson, Miami Beach, Florida, December 18, 1994. The author has written a commentary on the hymn that is included in *Global Praise 1, Resource Book*, available from GBGMusik.

Theme: In this text the author mirrors all the children of the world in diverse contexts through the life of the Star-Child, Jesus. Stanzas 1 and 5 emphasize the identity of God's gift of the Star-Child, and stanzas 2-4 reflect the children of the world to whom Jesus has come to give abundant life. The refrain is a plea or prayer that every year Christmas will come to all people, namely, that the divine love revealed in Jesus will fill the lives of people wherever they are and in whatever condition they find themselves.

Liturgical use: The song is appropriate for Advent and Christmas worship and celebration. It may also be used for baptisms, particularly infant baptisms.

Performance and style: Do not rush the song. It may have varied presentations: soloist, congregation, choir, or combinations of any of these. Tempo: quarter note = 88-92.

Instrumentation: The song may be accompanied by a keyboard instrument, guitar, bass, flute, organ, etc.

Teaching tips: To understand the author's development of the text, first read and sing the refrain. Ask members of the group what they think the author means by "let the day arrive when Christmas comes for every one, everyone alive." After some discussion, have the group sing stanza 1, followed by soloists singing stanzas 2-4. Everyone sings the refrain following each stanza. Everyone sings stanza 5, beginning very softly and building to the refrain, and continuing more quietly to the end. The refrain may be repeated or quietly hummed. Ask members of the group for reflections on the metaphors and descriptions of children, all kinds from all places.

References: In the Appendix of the *Global Praise 1* songbook, there are additional versions of the song in German (40a-1), Spanish (40a-2), and Korean (40a-3). The song is recorded on *Global Praise 1* (CD 1-003, GBGMusik) and on the CD *Ninive* (Verlag Singende Gemeinde, Wuppertal, Germany). An anthem (SATB) setting by the composer is available from Hope Publishers, Carol Stream, Illinois, and another SATB arrangement for choir and keyboard is available in German from Verlag Singende Gemeinde (Wuppertal, Germany). The song is published in *EM* (2002).

41, ¡Miren qué bueno! / O look and wonder

Words: Adapted from Psalm 133 by Pablo Sosa, b. 1933, Argentina
Composer: Pablo Sosa
Background: The song was written for a local parish meeting of the whole congregation (kindergartners to grandparents) stressing the sense of communion.
Theme: The song describes communion as related to everyday, common pleasures.
Liturgical use: It is especially good as a gathering song, but otherwise it has multiple uses: as a hymn for Christian unity, on World Communion Sunday, and in ecumenical worship services and gatherings.
Performance and style: Sing it joyfully but not too fast. This is a *chamarrita* from the eastern area of Argentina and Uruguay. Watch for the triplets in the stanzas. The dynamic level is *mezzo forte.* Tempo: quarter note = 84.
Instrumentation: Guitar, piano
Reference: It is recorded on *Éste es el Día: Canciones de Pablo Sosa,* a product of ISEDET (Buenos Aires, Argentina).

42, Oré poriajú verekó / O Lord, have mercy

Author/Composer: Anonymous
Background: This song is presented as sung in Catholic Masses in Paraguay. It was first transcribed by Pablo Sosa at the General Assembly of the Latin American Council of Churches, Indaiatuba, Brazil, 1988, when it was introduced by a group of delegates from Paraguay.
Theme: The words are the Guaraní version of the Greek *kyrie eleison,* made by the Jesuit missionaries in colonial times. Guarani is

spoken in Paraguay (where, together with Spanish, it is the official language) and in northeastern Argentina. The Guaraní culture is one of the most important in the southern part of South America. The literal translation is as follows: *Oré* (we, us) *poriajú* (mercy), *verekó* (have), *ñandeyara* (God). The music is contemporary, using the *guarania* rhythm created by the well-known Paraguayan composer José Asunción Flores in 1925.

Liturgical use: It may be used for the *kyrie eleison* in the service of Holy Communion, and also as a prayer response.

Style and performance: The rhythm should be steady and flowing, not rushed. Tempo: quarter note = 68.

Instrumentation: Guitar, piano

Reference: It is published in *EM* (2002) and recorded on *Tenemos Esperanza* (CD 1-016, GBGMusik) and on *Du bist der Atem meiner Lieder* (Anker Musik, Germany).

43, Laudate omnes gentes / Sing praises, all you peoples

Text: Psalm 117

Composer: Jacques Berthier, b. 1923, d. 1994, France

Background: This is a setting of the opening statement of Psalm 117 by the French composer Jacques Berthier for the Taizé community. See *GP2,* #127, for more information on the composer..

Theme: This song is an exhortation to all peoples and nations to praise God.

Liturgical use: This song is particularly useful at the beginning of worship. Its quiet, insistent energy is very helpful in fostering and establishing a focused, worshipful mood.

Performance and style: As with most Taizé chants, this song should be repeated *ad libitum* as many times as necessary for the congregation to engage profoundly in its call to worship God. It should be sung in a quiet, legato, unrushed fashion. The congregation should be encouraged to sing in parts. A quiet chordal accompaniment may be provided by guitar, piano, or organ, with *obbligato* instrumental parts interspersed. Make sure the accompaniment is simple and does not compete with the vocal parts. Tempo: quarter note = ca. 66.

Teaching tips: Sing in a flowing, uninterrupted manner with clear phrases articulated every two measures. Make sure that there is no delay from the end of a phrase to the beginning of the next.

References: The song is published in *EM* (2002). Further choral and
instrumental parts for this song may be found in *Music from Taizé*,
Vol. 1, published by GIA Publications, Inc. (7404 So. Mason Ave.,
Chicago, IL 60638, 800-442-1358, 800 442-1358).

44, Vi vill ha fred / Longing for peace

Author/Composer: Per Harling, b. 1948, Sweden

Background: This simple and playful song was written for a special
peace service in Sweden, to which people of all ages were invited.
The song was composed for the sermon, in which Pastor Harling
talked about the difference between finding peace with yourself
(often quite easy!) and peace with your neighbor (more difficult!).

Theme: Become involved in peacemaking as a follower of Christ.

Liturgical use: In any service, especially where children are part of
the congregation, and where peace issues are introduced. It is
appropriate for ecumenical services and Holy Communion.

Performance and style: The song is short and thus very easy to learn by
heart in a short time. Sing it over and over again, clapping your hands
at the right places, until you find that people know it without using the
music. Do not immediately ask the people to join hands. When they
know the song from memory, have them join hands at the end.
However, do not sing the final line until all have joined their hands.
Now tell the people to keep their hands joined and sing the song once
more, asking them to clap their neighbors' hands (not their own hands)
this time. Listen to the clapping sound and compare it to the sound
of people clapping their own hands. There is always a big difference.
When you clap your own hands, you know how to do it because you
have practiced it many times, but when you have to find your
neighbor's hand in order to clap it with your hand, it is much more
difficult. This exercise may lead to a good discussion about peace
work. It needs practice!

Now repeat the song and the clapping sequence. The first time
through, clap your own hands (listening to the "right" clapping
sound), and the second time clap your neighbor's hands; by the very
end all hands may be raised, symbolizing the uniting of everyone.
Tempo: quarter note = 70.

Instrumentation: It may be sung *a cappella* or with keyboard instruments,
guitar, bass, and percussion.

45, Tino tenda Jesu / Thank you, Jesus, amen

Author/Arranger: Patrick Matsikenyiri, b. 1937, Zimbabwe
Background: Thanksgiving for what the Lord has done and will continue
  to do is at the heart of African people. In Zimbabwe, The United
  Methodist Church has established July as the "Harvest Thanksgiving
  month," when people bring offerings of money and the products of
  their labor.
Theme: Thanksgiving
Liturgical use: It is appropriate for all services of thanksgiving and
  gratitude or moments in liturgies where thanksgiving is expressed, e.g.,
  the offertory.
Performance and style: Though it is straightforward, the leader may
  embellish the melody according to his or her skill to add vitality to the
  song. Tempo: quarter note = 84.
Teaching tips: Speak the text clearly and encourage people to sing it in the
  original Shona language.
Reference: It is recorded on *Youth Mission Chorale: Asia Tour 2001*
  (CD 1-020, GBGMusik).

46, Muchindikani Yesu / Come, let us honor Jesus

Author/Composer: Tumbuka hymn by Ben Nhlane, d. 1910[?],
  Malawi; language, Ngoni; Eng. trans., Max Jawati
Background and theme: The mood represents that of the wedding
  ceremony and celebration. The leader/response pattern gives the song
  vitality, especially if the bass line supports it with vigor. Welcoming
  the coming of Jesus as a groom marks the primary theological
  emphasis of the song.
Theme: Believers in Jesus Christ greet their Savior and are reminded to
  heed his call to follow and to bring their burdens and hearts to him.
Liturgical use: It is appropriate for weddings, Christmas, Palm Sunday,
  and any other events which emphasize commitment to Christ and
  following in his way.
Performance and style: The English stanzas may be used in accordance
  with the need of the choir and congregation. A mixture of English and
  the original language would also be effective. Tempo: dotted quarter
  note = 84.
Reference: It is recorded on *Africa Praise 1* (CD 1-004, GBGMusik) and

on *Youth Mission Chorale: Asia Tour 2001* (CD 1-020, GBGMusik).

47, Sing welcome to our Savior

Author: Thomas Stevenson Colvin, Scotland, b. 1925, d. 2000
Composer: Based on the Tumbuka hymn by Ben Nhlane
Background: The author spent over thirty years in Africa as a missionary
of the Presbyterian Church of Scotland and developed a passion for
the music of the continent and the needs of the people. In many texts,
as in this one, he shaped what he heard and experienced in the daily
lives of African peoples, including their deepest yearnings and needs.
While Colvin shaped the text in his own words, they resonate from the
heart of Africa and its many peoples.
Theme: The community of faith greets the Savior, Jesus Christ, whose
saving action to free humankind from sin and fear also brings the
advent of justice, the liberation of captives, and freedom from the reign
of tyrants.
Liturgical use: Holy Communion, World Communion Sunday,
Reformation Day, Christmas, Easter, Pentecost
Performance and style: It may be sung in a call-and-response format.
Tempo: dotted quarter note = 84.

48, My Lord! What a morning

Text/Music: Unknown, African American Spiritual; arr., Melva A.
Costen, b. 1933, USA
Background and theme: The dawning of a new day, a day marked by
universal justice as envisioned in a number of scriptural texts, is one
way of affirming the hope of the gospel. For Africans enslaved in
America, a vision of the cataclysmic destruction of the earth where
elements of the creation process are turned upside down provide a
starting point for better days ahead. The language of the refrain of this
spiritual is based on references in the Old Testament (e.g., Isaiah
13:10; Joel 2:10-11) and in the New Testament to stars of the sky
falling to the earth (Revelation 6:12-17; Matthew 24:29). This kind of
eruption in the order of creation will announce the beginning of a new
day and will mysteriously cause the last trumpet to resound with such
volume that it could surely wake the dead who are already alive in
Christ. Some interpreters of this spiritual extend the signs of hope to

the Day of Judgment and the Second Coming of Christ from these words of Jesus: "And then all the tribes of the earth will *mourn* and they will see the Son of Man coming on the clouds of heaven with power and great glory" (Matthew 24:30). Thus, both *mourning* and *morning* are appropriate reminders of the beginning of a great day of justice.[2]

The three stanzas (you will hear "the trumpet sound," "the sinner cry," and "the Christian shout") are used in most published versions. However, in some congregations where the spiritual-singing tradition has been continuous, one may hear additional stanzas such as "the moaning sound," "the battle cry," "marching feet," or other more contemporary expressions.

When stanzas are added, they can be introduced by a soloist as a "call," with the familiar line following as if in response to the call.

Liturgical Use: This spiritual is appropriate for the Advent season and on any occasion in connection with the scriptural passages cited above, e.g., the lectionary, that support the text of the song.

Performance, style, and teaching tips: The simplicity of the melody allows this spiritual to be taught either by rote or from the score. Once the melody is repeated several times, the assembly should be able to hear the harmonic flow or to learn the parts from the score. Advanced choirs will find the tonal paintings in the chromatic progressions exciting. Tempo: quarter note = 76.

49, Santo, santo, santo / Holy, holy, holy

Author/Composer: Anonymous; harm., Carlton R. Young, b. 1926, USA

Background: The song appears here as sung in charismatic meetings in Argentina, where the influence of music from the USA is predominant.

Theme: The text includes an interesting combination of the transcendent character of the Creator God as expressed in the "three times holy" invocation, and the immanent God whose love we confess most intimately (and sentimentally).

Liturgical use: The song has multiple uses. It is often sung as the *sanctus* of the Eucharist, but the mood of the music needs a very special introduction in order not to come to an anticlimax after the words "Therefore with angels and archangels, and the whole company of heaven," etc.

Performance and style: Sing slowly, but do not drag. Tempo: quarter note

= 66-76. The presentation should be very flexible—*espressivo*. Sing evenly without giving undue stress to syllables or individual notes. Move from *mezzo piano* to *piano* to *pianissimo*.

Instrumentation: organ, piano, guitar, solo voices, etc.

Teaching tips: Try "drawing" the melodic line in the air with your hands, following the height of each one of the notes. The movements may become quite meaningful as you descend with the words "holy," for instance, or as you ascend with the words "my heart."

Reference: It is recorded on *Youth Mission Chorale: Asia Tour 2001* (CD 1-020, GBGMusik). The recorded choral arrangement is available in the *GP Choral Series* (CS 1005). The song is published in *EM* (2002) and in *MV* (2002).

50, Ocean of love

Author/Composer: M. Thomas Thangaraj, b. 1942, India

Background: This song was composed with congregational singing in mind. Each line may be sung by a leader and immediately repeated by the congregation.

Theme: The theme is set in relation to the South Indian piety of praising God by ascribing many and varied names to God, such as "Ocean of love, Fountain of joy, Light of justice."

Liturgical use: This piece may be sung as an invocation, a response to a litany or prayers, and/or a hymn for Holy Communion.

Performance and style: Sing in a slow tempo to the accompaniment of a drone consisting of the first and fifth notes of the scale (in this case, C and G). The drone may be played on the organ or on any keyboard by sustaining the two notes. Or two bell players may strike these two notes at the beginning of each bar. The leader sings each line, and the congregation repeats after the leader. The piece is set in the *raga* (scale) called *thodi*, consisting of the following notes: C, Db, Eb, F, G, Ab, Bb, and C. Tempo: quarter note = 58-62. This is equivalent of the Phrygian mode, which begins and ends on the third degree of a major scale.

Teaching tips: First, sing the notes in the *raga*. Then ask the people to sing the melody before one begins to sing the entire song. They may hum or use the syllables "la, oo, ah." Since the people repeat after the leader, not much rehearsal is needed to sing this piece.

Reference: It is recorded with flute accompaniment on *Youth Praise:*

European Tour 1998 (CD 1-010, GBGMusik).

51, O many people of all lands

Author: Natty G. Barranda, b. 1940, Philippines; professor at Xenia
    University, Ohio, USA
Composer: Lois F. Bello, b. 1930, Philippines
Background: The author, originally from the Philippines, is a professor at
    Xenia University in Ohio. As one who lives across cultures, she
    expresses confidence in the inclusiveness of the God of all cultures
    and in the inclusiveness of God's people.
Theme: Praising God, God of all cultures, thank offering, trust,
    assurance, commitment
Liturgical use: It is appropriate as a call to worship, thanksgiving,
    offering, sending forth. During the liturgical year, it may have general
    use but is also fitting for Pentecost, World Communion Sunday and
    regular Eucharistic celebrations.
Performance and style: Minor mode, triple time, with an occasional
    switch of accent to the second beat (measure 10) and sudden
    modulation to its tonic major (measures 8-9) are special features of
    contemporary Filipino style with early Spanish influence. It would
    sound more Filipino with a guitar accompaniment. Tempo: quarter
    note = 126-132.
Teaching tips: Notice the sudden change of time in measure 3 and the
    interplay between F minor and F major, which is typical of Filipino
    style. Avoid conducting in three; it would be more effective swinging
    in a circular motion (one for each measure) to let the music flow.

52, O thou who this mysterious bread

Author: Charles Wesley, b. 1707, d. 1788, Great Britain
Composer: Unknown; music, LAND OF REST, Southern USA folk song
Background and theme: The hymn text first appeared in *Hymns on the
    Lord's Supper*, 1745, and is based on the disciples' Emmaus
    encounter with the risen Christ, Luke 24:13-35. LAND OF REST is
    adapted from *The Christian Harp*, 1832, 1836 edition. Stanzas 2 and 3
    may be sung as a canon, or round, begun by men's voices, and treble
    voices entering at beat six of the next measure. The first use of this
    tune with the Wesley text appeared in *The United Methodist Hymnal*

(1989).

Theme: The hymn is an invitation from the faithful to the risen Lord to speak words of grace and feed their souls with God's gifts of mercy, pardon, and love.

Liturgical use: Holy Communion

Performance, style, and instrumentation: I may be sung with keyboard instruments, piano, or organ, but it is also very effective when sung *a cappella* using the SATB scoring found in *Global Praise 2.* Tempo: dotted half note = 54.

53, The golden rule she has pursued

Author: Charles Wesley, b. 1707, d. 1788, Great Britain
Composer: Samuel Sebastian Wesley, b. 1766, d. 1837
Background: The stanzas for this hymn were selected by S T Kimbrough, Jr., from the poem "On the death of Mrs. Mary Naylor, March 21st, 1757," which was published in Charles Wesley's *Journal.*[3] Stanza 1 is from Part II (original stanza 3); stanzas 2-3 are from Part III (original stanzas 2-4); stanza 5 is from Part I (original stanza 2). It was often Charles Wesley's practice on the occasion of someone's death to write a poetical tribute to the deceased person. Often they were, as was Mary Naylor, everyday saints who bore in their posture the Lamb of God.

   The tune CORNWALL was first published in *The European Psalmist* (1872), as a setting for Charles Wesley's hymn "Thou God of glorious majesty." It became better known however, after it appeared in *Hymns Ancient and Modern* where it was used for "O Love divine, how sweet thou art." The tune's first use with "The golden rule she has pursued was in *A Song for the Poor* (New York: General Board of Global Ministries, 1993), reprinted as *Songs for the Poor* (1997).

Theme: One celebrates the life of Mary Naylor, who modeled the way the followers of Jesus should live out justice, reaching out to the destitute, sick, and imprisoned. One should keep her life in view and hence so live.

Liturgical use: Liturgies with the themes of justice and service to the marginalized are appropriate for this hymn. It is an excellent hymn at Holy Communion.

Performance and style: It may be sung *a cappella,* especially if introduced and supported by a choir. Organ or keyboard is also appropriate. Stanza 2 could be sung as a solo, stanza 3 by the women, stanza 4 by the men, and all joining in on stanzas 1 and 5. Tempo: quarter note = 96-112.

54, Your duty let th'apostle show

Author: Charles Wesley, b. 1707, d. 1788, Great Britain
Composer: Timothy Edward Kimbrough, b. 1957, USA
Background: This hymn setting was composed for use as a congregational hymn. When the GBGMusik songbook *Songs for the Poor*
(1993) was being prepared, the editor asked the composer to write
a musical setting for an 8.8.6.8.8.6 meter poem. This was a meter used
often by Charles Wesley and was quite common in German-language
hymnody. Most English-language hymnbooks today, however, have
very few hymn tunes appropriate for this meter. The Wesley poem
remained unpublished until 1990, when S T Kimbrough, Jr. and Oliver
A. Beckerlegge included it in vol. 2 of *The Unpublished Poetry of
Charles Wesley* (Nashville: Abingdon./Kingswood).
Theme: The primary themes are discipleship and the church triumphant.
This text describes as well as any from Charles Wesley's pen the
intimate relationship between personal and social holiness, personal
piety and acts of mercy and justice.
Liturgical use: The hymn may be sung at any time in most any church
assembly. It is particularly appropriate for stewardship and commitment.
Performance and style: Do not rush the hymn. The words are extremely
important. Note the breath mark in the penultimate measure; hold
almost as a *fermata.* The break is intentional so as to give one time to
consider the affirmation at the end of each stanza about what one may
do in response to God. Tempo: quarter note = 96-112.
Instrumentation: The hymn is best suited for accompaniment by organ or
piano.
Reference: It is recorded on *Songs for the Poor* (CD 1-001, GBGMusik).

55, Peace is my last gift to you

Text: John 14:27; *The Book of Common Prayer,* 1979
Composer: Timothy Edward Kimbrough, b. 1957, USA
Background: This setting of John 14:27 was composed for use as a
foot-washing anthem at the Maundy Thursday liturgy.

Theme: The primary themes are discipleship and servant-hood.

Liturgical use: The Book of Common Prayer (1979) assigns this text for reading or singing during the foot-washing of the Maundy Thursday liturgy of Holy Week. It may also enjoy use as a congregational response to the celebrant's offering of the peace in the Eucharistic assembly. Some may find it useful as a benediction.

Performance and style: The *Global Praise 1: Program and Resource Book* includes a complete setting of stanzas, which may be sung by a choir after each singing of the chorus by the congregation. Tempo: quarter note = 96.

56, Shukuru Allah / Let the people know

Author/Composer: Unknown

Background: This particular Christian song is written in a southern Sudanese dialect, which is a *patois* of Arabic and a local dialect. The range of musical notes from "D" to "B" is the range of many Arabic chants. Hence the musical form originates from within the musical culture of the people.

Theme: This is a song of witness to Christ and the church, a bold affirmation for those who sing it in a context that has not always been friendly to Christian witness. The opening word *shukuru* originates from the Arabic word *shukran*, meaning "thanks." The opening line could also be translated "Thanks to God, Allah, messengers are present here."

Liturgical use: This is an effective song for services with themes of evangelism and mission, liturgies of commissioning and ordination.

Performance and style: Sing *a cappella;* the use of percussion instruments is appropriate, providing they are not played too elaborately. Use a simple but steady rhythm.

Reference: It is recorded on *Youth Mission Chorale: Asia Tour 2001* (CD 1-020, GBGMusik), and included in *GP Choral Series, African Medley 2* (CS 1003).

57, Salvation, there's no better word

Author: Fred Pratt Green, b. 1903, d. 2000, United Kingdom

Composer: Joseph Barnby, b. 1838, d. 1896, Great Britain

Background: The text was written by Fred Pratt Green. When editing the *Global Praise 1* songbook, S T Kimbrough, Jr., thought it important to include a hymn of Fred Pratt Green, which would reflect his significant contribution to English-language hymnody in the second half of the twentieth century. This particular text of Pratt Green at the time of the publication of the *Global Praise 1* songbook had never been set to music. Kimbrough selected the Barnby tune and the result was the hymn as it appears in *GP1*. See also the musical setting of Ivor H. Jones in the Appendix of the *GP1* songbook at 57(a).

Theme: The three stanzas are an excellent summary of a Wesleyan perspective of what God has done for all in Jesus Christ. God's act of Incarnation in Jesus Christ is an act of personal redemption. It is what Christ has done "for me." But it is also an act of corporate redemption. It is what Christ has done "for us." The barriers between all human beings are broken down, and God's love breaks through into human hearts.

Liturgical use: It is appropriate for general services throughout the year and especially for evangelism emphases.

Performance and style: Sing with piano/organ accompaniment or *a cappella* in the four-part harmonization of Barnby. Tempo: half note = 60.

Reference: See *GP1* Appendix 57(a) for an alternate setting.

58, Still for thy lovingkindness

Author: Charles Wesley, b. 1707, d. 1788, Great Britain
Composer: Swee-Hong Lim, b. 1963, Singapore
Background: This hymn was originally scored as a choral anthem and was used by the composer for his Baccalaureate recital. It was subsequently rescored as a hymn for congregational worship.
Theme: Anticipation of the presence of God in worship
Liturgical Use: Lent, service music for intercessory prayer, Holy Communion
Performance and style: This hymn may be sung unaccompanied. If accompaniment is needed, keep it very simple. Do not rush the tempo. The dynamics should be plaintive and quiet. Tempo: quarter note = 68.
Instrumentation: Keep all accompaniment austere and simple, e.g., use a recorder instead of a piano where possible. The recorder should be played heterophonically, i.e., with slight improvisation along the melodic line. Add grace notes where appropriate, e.g., at the end of phrases.

Teaching tips: Play the tune using a single wind instrument (e.g., recorder, oboe, or flute). Following this, the leader can gently guide the congregation in its singing by minute hand gestures indicating melodic pitches and the contour of the musical phrase.

Reference: A choral arrangement of moderate difficulty for this work is available in the *GP Choral Series* (WS 2006) and is recorded on the accompanying CD *Anthem Sampler.* A congregational version with organ and oboe accompaniment is also available. It is recorded also on the CD *Du bist der Atem meiner Lieder* (Anker Musik, Stuttgart, Germany). The song is published in *EM* (2002) with German translation. See *GP1* Appendix 58(a) for Chinese (Mandarin) text.

59, Tenemos esperanza / We have hope

Author: Federico J. Pagura, b. 1923, Argentina
Composer: Homero Perera, b. 1939, Argentina
Background and theme: Bishop Frederico J. Pagura, an early leader of the Ecumenical Movement for Human Rights in Argentina, is the author of this powerful text. Set to Perera's music, this outcry of the people of Latin America has become a banner song in their struggle for justice and peace. Homero Perera, the composer, set the text to a musical idiom, the *tango,* hitherto restricted to dance halls, and hence avoided by Protestants. During the series of dictatorships in Argentina from 1976 to 1983, this song, with its indictment of the powers of oppression coupled with an emphasis on the hope of God's people, became a witness to the suffering and struggle of the *Madres de la Plaza de Mayo,* a group of mothers who continue through nonviolent means to demand information regarding their children who disappeared during the period of the above-mentioned dictatorships.

    The song is a marvelous example of the uniting of what was considered to be an evil force, the *tango,* with the message of hope to illustrate the biblical reality that God takes what people often perceive as the worst to make of it an instrument for justice and truth.

Liturgical use: General use, ecumenical gatherings and worship services, Christmas, Epiphany
Performance and style: The music is written in the style of *tango.* Tempo: quarter note = 88.
Instrumentation: piano, guitar, bass guitar, violin, drums, and percussion instruments

Teaching tips: Teach the refrain of the song first. Play and sing the melody line only. Once the congregation is secure with the melody, have a choir or soloist sing the stanzas. Invite everyone to join at the chorus.

Reference: A recording of the song is available on *Tenemos Esperanza* (CD 1-016, GBGMusik) and on *Faith•Hope• Love* (CD 1-013, GBGMusik).

60, The right hand of God

Author: Patrick Prescod, b. 1932, St. Vincent
Composer: Noel Dexter, b. 1938, Jamaica
Background and theme: Prescod (music teacher and now retired organist of Kingstown Methodist Church in the Caribbean Island of Saint Vincent) and Dexter (Musical Director at the University of the West Indies, Mona Campus, Kingston, Jamaica) have captured the true Caribbean spirit in this hymn. Composed as a theme song for the Inaugural Ceremony of the Caribbean Conference of Churches in 1973, it uses the image of God's right hand, the symbol of power. Psalm 98:1 states: "His right hand and his holy arm have gotten him victory." There is the expressed conviction that God is very much involved in the history of the Caribbean and that with God's help, the islands of the region can grow from strength to strength. God is ever present, making a claim upon our lives, and guides, uplifts the fallen, wipes out evil, and heals broken bodies, minds, and souls.

Liturgical use: It is appropriate for the opening and closing of worship, and for services of justice and reconciliation

Performance and style: The music follows a typical Jamaican folk pattern using dotted crotchets. The syncopation is distinctively Caribbean and is characteristic of the *calypso* style. Tempo: half note = 84..

Instrumentation: Suggested accompaniment: piano, guitar, bass guitar, violin, drums, and percussion instruments.

Teaching tips: The song is best taught to congregations at a slow tempo, then gradually, as the singers gain confidence with the words and melody, the tempo can be increased to *calypso* speed.

Reference: It is recorded on *Caribbean Praise* (CD 1-011, GBGMusik).

61, Tuyo es el Reino / Yours is the Kingdom

Words: Gospel of Matthew

Composer: Pablo Sosa, b. 1933, Argentina

Background and theme: The song was written ca. 1978, and its first performance was in English at the World Mission and Evangelism Conference, Melbourne, Australia, 1980. The music grew out of the composer's desire to be able to sing this doxology, which was added by the early Christians to the Lord's Prayer.

Liturgical use: The song has multiple liturgical uses, e.g., the Festival of Christ the King, Advent, Christmas; prayer response and with The Lord's Prayer.

Performance and style: The first time through, sing it slowly and somewhat heavily, stressing each note in the style of the *baguala,* from Northern Argentina and Bolivia. *Accellerando* towards the end and sing it a second time vigorously, *forte.* Maintain a stesdy beat.

Instrumentation: Guitar, drum, flute

Reference: It is recorded on *Éste es el Día: Canciones de Pablo Sosa,* a product of ISEDET (Buenos Aires, Argentina).

62, O moi, Gospod / To you, O God

Author: Andrei Igorevitch Lukashin, b. 1964, Russia; Eng. paraphrase, S T Kimbrough, Jr., b. 1936, USA

Composer: Ludmila Garbuzova, b. 1948, Russia; arr., Carlton R. Young, b. 1926, USA

Background and theme: Andrei Lukashin is a pastor and writer of the Russian Presbyterian Church. This is a prayer of repentance. It is one of the author's first lyrics and one of the composer's first songs, because a prayer of repentance is the first step for every Christian. It is based on Psalm 25:11, "For your name's sake, O Lord, pardon my iniquity, for it is great!"

Liturgical use: It is especially appropriate for Holy Communion and prayer services. May be used as a prayer of confession.

Performance and style: The style is that of a traditional Russian song. It is not to be sung too fast but with much feeling and *rubati.* Tempo: 84-88. Increase the tempo gradually—*ad libitum poco a poco accelerando.* The dynamics of the song move from double *pianissimo* to *forte* at "alleluia."

Instrumentation: It may be accompanied by piano or guitar.

Teaching tips: (1) Hum the melody through. (2) Read the text together in the rhythm of song. (3) Sing the song very slowly and quietly with a keyboard. (4) When teaching non-Russian language singers, sing in English, but learn the single Russian phrase in each stanza which follows the "alleluia." See Appendix 62(a) for a romanized transliteration of the text.

References: It is recorded on *Russian Praise* (CD 1-007, GBGMusik) and *Global Praise 1* (CD 1-003, GBGMusik). See *GP1* Appendix 62(a) for Russian (Cyrillic) text and Romanized transliteration.

63, Truly baptized into the name

Author: Charles Wesley, b. 1707, d. 1788, Great Britain
Composer: S T Kimbrough, Jr., b. 1936, USA; harm., Mary K. Jackson, b. 1934, USA
Background: This is one Wesley's previously unpublished texts. (See *The Unpublished Poetry of Charles Wesley,* 3 Vols., edited by S T Kimbrough, Jr., and Oliver A. Beckerlegge (Nashville: Kingswood, 1988, 1990, 1992); Vol. 2, *Hymns on the Holy Scriptures.* Wesley often wrote sacred hymns and poems while reflecting on passages of Scripture. This particular hymn is based on Acts 19:5, "They were baptized in the name of the Lord Jesus."
Theme: At baptism, one becomes a partner of the nature of Jesus Christ and experiences the full salvation of God for eternity.
Liturgical use: The hymn is fitting for all services of baptism.
Performance and style: Have the choir or congregation sing the hymn at the time of the presentation of infants for baptism. The hymn could also be sung *a cappella* in the SATB voicing found at #63. Tempo: quarter note = 110-120.
Instrumentation: There are two keyboard versions in the *Global Praise 1* songbook. The first is at number 63 and the other at 63(a) in the Appendix. Piano, organ, or other keyboard may be used. However, the setting in the Appendix includes the chords for guitar. Harp or keyboard could also be used for accompaniment.
Teaching tips: The melodic line is very simple and, if sung or played through on an instrument, the congregation will immediately pick up the melody.

64, Wa wa wa emimimo / Come, O Holy Spirit, come

Author/Composer: Unknown; origin: Church of the Lord (Aladura),

Nigeria; language: Yoruba

Background and theme: As events unfold in the world, the yearning for the Holy Spirit to intervene becomes more apparent. Christians around the world have realized that nothing short of God's divine intervention can succeed amid such turmoil. Therefore this song reflects the constant summoning of the Holy Spirit to deliver all humankind from evil.

Liturgical use: It is appropriate for Pentecost and as a call to worship but may also be used for intercessory prayer.

Performance and style: Work on the men's part first. Remind the choir that as long as the men sing their part at the end of the lines, the song continues. When ending the song, the men omit "Emimimo." Try the Yoruba language first, then the Shona language, then English, and perhaps return to Yoruba at the end. Tempo: quarter note = 88-96.

Movements: Extend the arms upward and bending them at the elbows bring the hands downward toward the head in the rhythm of the song to indicate the summoning of the Holy Spirit. When the song is used as a processional, make gestures that invite the congregation in the pews to move from side to side.

Teaching tips: Make sure the men's part is vibrant. Tenor voices may add embellishments.

Reference: It is recorded on *Africa Praise 1* (CD 1-004, GBGMusik). It appears in the *GP Choral Series* in *African Medley 1* (CS 1002), and in *MV* (2002).

65, Tua palavra na vida / Your word in our lives

Author/Composer: Simei Monteiro, b. 1943, Brazil; trans., Jorge Rodríguez (Spanish) / Sonya Ingwersen (English)

Background: The Bible presents several images or metaphors for "Word of God." This hymn uses some of these images present in the Bible such as: fountain, water, seed, mirror, sharp sword, and light. These metaphors are a contrast to the second part of each stanza that describes a very concrete situation in which the Word can be incarnated or can give new meaning to life.

Theme: The Word is a guide for our daily life. It is an affirmation of faith in the power of the Word of God and the belief that we must live according to it.

Liturgical use: Acclamation of the Word, prayer service, Sunday School, confessional services, or during sermons

Performance and style: This style is adapted from an old-fashioned *modinha.* Pay attention to the augmented fourth interval between measures 2 and 3. The song is conducted more easily if felt in 6/8. Tempo: quarter note = 120.

Instrumentation: Use guitar or piano. A flute introduction and descant may be added.

Teaching tips: Play with the augmented fourth interval, repeating it a number of times. Afterwards the melody is easily sung. The meditative character will be highlighted.

66, When our lives know sudden shadow

Author: Shirley Erena Murray, b. 1931, New Zealand

Composer: Carlton R. Young, b. 1926, USA

Background: Carlton R. Young composed the tune for the memorial service of a person who died of HIV/AIDS and whose first name is the tune name, RODNEY. The family was in denial regarding the circumstances of the death. The mother wrote to the composer that the hymn brought them together as a family, allowing them to express their grief by reading and hearing the words while the music was played.

Theme: Compassion and assurance in times of grief, pain, loss, and sorrow

Performance and style: Suggestion for performance: stanzas 1 and 4 may be sung by all voices; stanza 2 by the women and stanza 3 by the men. Tempo: half note = 68-72.

Instrumentation: Organ and piano are appropriate.

Reference: It is recorded on *New Beginnings: The Music of Carlton R. Young* (CD 1-018, GBGMusik) and on *Faith•Hope•Love* (CD 1-013, GBGMusik), on the CD *Meine Zeit in Gottes Händen* (Verlag Singende Gemeinde, Wuppertal, Germany). See *GP1* Appendix 66(a-1) for a Korean translation and romanized transliteration, and 66(a-2) for a Spanish translation. It is published in *EM* (2002) and in a German-language SATB choral arrangement (Verlag Singende Gemeinde, Wuppertal, Germany).

67, Tuya es la Gloria / We sing of your glory

Author/Composer: Unknown; words based on Revelation 4:11; harm., Carlton R. Young, b. 1926, USA

Background: The song appears here as it is sung in charismatic meetings in Argentina, where the influence of music from US evangelical song is predominant.

Theme: The words celebrate the power of God.

Liturgical use: The song is applicable and adaptable to many different liturgical contexts. It is especially appropriate after prayers of thanksgiving or testimonies of God's power; as an opening hymn of praise, hymn of dedication, or hymn to accompany times of prayer.

Performance and style: A slow but flowing tempo of quarter note = 76-84 is recommended. Change the accompaniment and texture of each stanza in order to emphasize the particular message of each. For example, sing the third stanza *a cappella,* and the fourth with keyboard or organ. Tempo: quarter note = 86.

Teaching tips: The sequential nature of this song's melody makes it very easy to teach. Usually the first stanza sung by a soloist or choir or played on a lead instrument should suffice for the song to be learned quickly.

Instrumentation: Guitar, piano, or organ

References: A choral version of the song for SATB voices is available in the *GP Choral Series* (CS 1018), and recorded on the accompanying CD *Anthem Sampler.* The song is published in *EM* (2002) and recorded in German on the CD *Dir, Gott, sei die Ehre* (Verlag Singende Gemeinde, Wuppertal, Germany).

68, Guide my feet

Author: Unknown, African American Spiritual

Composer: Willis Laurence James, b. 1900, d. 1966, USA; arr. Wendell Whalum, b. 1932, d. 1986, USA

Background and theme: This is an African American spiritual, which by virtue of its definition as a religious folksong, was shaped and expressed by the slave community that created it. The scriptural inspiration for this song is perhaps Hebrews 12:1-2: "Since we are surrounded by so great a cloud of witnesses, let us lay aside every weight . . . and let us run with perseverance the race that is set before us, looking to Jesus the pioneer and perfecter of our faith." According to the oral tradition, this is one of the spirituals that has dual meaning. On the one hand, it is a reminder that the vast community of the faithful now in the presence of the Almighty continually supports the earthly efforts to persevere as Christians. Couched in this Pauline metaphor is a message to the slave community to persevere and keep steadfast in the race it is running toward earthly freedom.

The tune is one of several available settings. This melody is from the 1984 collection of spirituals by Willis Laurence James and harmonized by the late-distinguished musician, Dr. Wendell Whalum, a native of Memphis, Tennessee, who was educated at Moorehouse College, Atlanta, Georgia, and the University of Iowa. He distinguished himself as organist, choral director, arranger, and head of the music department at Moorehouse College, positions which he held until his death.

Liturgical use: This spiritual can be used at any place in the service in response to the Word, which calls the community to run the race, knowing that the spiritual race is not in vain. It is especially appropriate during services of baptism and ordination. It may also be used as a hymn for sending forth, and services celebrating peace and justice.

Performance and style: The manner of performance in worship depends largely upon its location in the liturgy (order of service). After an energetic sermon about running the race with perseverance, the community's use of this spiritual in response will be upbeat and enthusiastic, accompanied by handclapping and bodily movement. As a closing hymn, it sends the community forth with the same kind of enthusiasm. It may be used as a contemplative benediction or response to other portions of the liturgy. Tempo: quarter note = 88-118.

Teaching tips: When teaching this spiritual, a keyboard accompaniment may be used to accentuate the melodic line. It may also be taught as a call-and-response song, with the first line reiterated in each stanza in unison. The structural pattern makes "Guide My Feet" extremely useful for a liturgical dance of the congregation and of small groups. Once the first stanza is learned, the community should sing all other stanzas in harmony as indicated in the score.

Reference: See *Global Praise 1: Program and Resource Book* (GBGMusik), p. 79, and Willis Laurence James, *Stars in the Elements: A Study of Negro Folk Music* (Athens: University of Georgia, 1984). The song is published in *EM* (2002).

Endnotes

1 Hugh Wybrew, *The Orthodox Liturgy: The Development of the Eucharistic Liturgy in the Byzantine Rite* (Crestwood, NY: St. Vladimir's Seminary Press, 1990), 77.

2 For an excellent interpretation of spirituals, see John Lovell, Jr., *Black Song: The Forge and the Flame* (New York: The Macmillan Company, 1972).

3 Thomas Jackson, *Journal of Charles Wesley*, 2 Vols., 2:338, 339, 341.

Global Praise 2

1, Yoeung mork chum knea chrieng / Hallelujah! We gather to sing God's praise

Author: Barnabas Mam, b. 1950, Cambodia; Eng. paraphrase, S T
  Kimbrough, Jr., b. 1936, USA
Composer: Anonymous
Background: Indigenous Cambodian Christian song was born ca. 1985
  among Cambodian Christians in refugee camps. One of its significant
  contributors is the Rev. Barnabas Mam, pastor of Church of the Living
  Hope in Phnom Penh, Cambodia. Mr. Sarin Sam, a Cambodian living
  in Australia, is, however, the primary creator of Cambodian Christian
  song. He has edited Cambodian hymnbooks for the Christian and
  Missionary Alliance and the churches of Methodism in Cambodia.

  The music of this well-known song was composed between 1950
  and 1955, but no one knows the name of the composer, only the title of
  the song, which translated mens "We are gathering to rejoice with all
  our hearts." Barnabas Mam understood the title as an expression of
  "hallelujah" and thus wrote the current text for the familiar melody.
Theme: The word "hallelujah" crosses all language boundaries and here
  expresses an overflowing of praise to the Creator God, the Holy
  Trinity, by the community of faith as it gathers for worship. The main
  theme of the song is that God is to be exalted and all people are to be
  joyful in God's presence.
Liturgical use: Introit, opening of worship
Performance and style: Handclapping and/or drumming on the beat is
  appropriate. The vocal style should be unison singing, which is the
  Khmer style. The rhythm is that of the Lao dance. When dancing to
  this rhythm, everyone is active and happy. The tempo should be
  lively: quarter note = 110.
Instrumentation: Use keyboards for rehearsal only; a flute may play the
  melody, and Asian drum(s) may be used. Young people today sometimes like to use brass, keyboard, and guitar.

2, Be silent

Author: Fanny Crosby, b. 1820, d.1915, USA. Her full name was
  Frances Jane Crosby.
Composer: William H. Doane, b. 1832, d. 1915, USA
Background and theme: The hymn is a call to prayer and worship. It

affirms that God speaks to individuals and to a congregation in worship. Fanny Crosby encourages silence as one enters a time of worship, for it is in the silence that one hears the words of God.

Liturgical use: It may be used as a call to worship, preparation for prayer, or a hymn sung prior to or during Holy Communion.

Performance and style: The hymn may be used for congregational singing, as a choral anthem, or as a solo. It is particularly effective sung *a cappella* in four-part harmony. All are acceptable styles of presentation. Tempo: quarter note = 80.

Instrumentation: One may use piano, organ, or subdued electronic keyboard.

3, Enter into Jerusalem

Author/Composer: Richard Ho Lung, b. 1939; arr., Patrick Prescod, b. 1932.

Background: The use of the Jamaican dialect, e.g., "mek we walk a-down there" (let us walk down there) makes this song one with which the people can immediately identity. Its exciting rhythm helps to remind Caribbean folk that they can worship God using the idioms that are common to their region.

Theme: The worship of God

Liturgical use: "Enter into Jerusalem" has been effectively used as a processional hymn either on the way to church or at the start of worship. It is ideal for church festivals, including Palm Sunday and Easter.

Performance and style: Worshippers are inclined not only to sing this song lustily but also to dance. Tempo: quarter note = 72-76.

Instrumentation: The accompaniment of piano, steel pan, guitars, drum set, and bass guitar can create an exciting atmosphere.

Teaching tips: When introducing this song, it is important to alert the singers to the expressions in the Jamaican dialect that do not conform to standard English, e.g. "we go celebrate" is a dialect form of saying" we are going to celebrate" or "we will celebrate."

Reference: It is recorded on *Caribbean Praise* (CD 1-011, GBGMusik).

4, Dzunzani Jehova / O praise God Jehovah

Author/Composer: Zacharias M. Uqueio, b. 1943, Mozambique; Eng.

paraphrase, S T Kimbrough, Jr., b. 1936, USA

Background: Xitswa is a tribal language of central Mozambique. Mr. Uqueio is a leader of church music in the United Methodist Church of Mozambique. The song was presented by Uqueio at the Global Praise Training Seminar, Candler School of Theology, Emory University, Atlanta, GA, USA, October 22-25, 1999.

Theme: Praise of God

Liturgical use: It is an excellent call to worship or call to praise.

Performance and style: The melody is in the upper voices throughout. In the stanzas, the men's voices accompany in chords, and in the refrain they sing rhythmic "hallelujahs." The song was transcribed by Carlton R. Young, who states, "The last three phrases of the refrain were not sung the same way twice, so it was difficult to put it into standard notation." Tempo: quarter note = 86.

Teaching tips: Teach the upper and lower parts separately.

5, Nzamuranza / I worship Christ

Author/Composer: Unknown; arr., Patrick Matsikenyiri, b. 1937, Zimbabwe; Eng. paraphrase, S T Kimbrough Jr., b. 1936, USA

Background: This is a hallelujah song or song of praise from Mozambique.

Theme: The song affirms the people's belief in Jesus, the resurrected Savior. He is unique and there is no one who can be compared to him. Therefore, the worshiper will praise him and make him the center of all adoration.

Liturgical use: The song may be used on all ocassions when songs of praise are appropriate. It is particularly fitting for the opening of worship services.

Performance and style: Sing vibrantly, especially when voicing the word "Hallelujah." People should feel free to sway joyfully with raised hands. The song follows a leader/response pattern. Tempo: quarter note = 116.

Instrumentation: Drum and *hosho* (shaker) are essential for instrumentation. A keyboard may be used to set people in motion, but it is optional after people have learned the song.

Teaching tips: Rehearse the last phrase for fluency in the original language or in English. If you sing in the original language, pronounce the "a" vowels as "ah," except "ay" is pronounced like the syllable "ny" in the word "deny." Tsah-moo-ran-tsah, ahngah-koh-nah-wah-koo-fah-nah nah-nayeh.

Reference: It is recorded by the African University Choir on the following GBGMusik recordings: *Africa Praise 1* (CD 1-004) and *Global Praise 2* (CD 1-012).

6, Aso, ngane Yesus / O come, all you people

Author/Composer: Unknown, Papua New Guinea; transcr./trans., I-to Loh, b. 1936, Taiwan

Background: The song was taught by a Roman Catholic priest at a conference in Manila, Philippines, in the mid-1980s, attended by I-to Loh.

Theme: The song stresses invitation to Christ and is a summons to worship.

Liturgical use: Call to worship; general use throughout the Christian year

Performance and style: The first time, it should be sung as a call by the leader, then the congregation responds and sings the second time through. Since the language is easy to pronounce, it would be better to sing in the original language. If desired, one can sing the English version the second time. Tempo: eighth note = ca. 58.

Instrumentation: An instrument may be used to introduce the melody, but after the song has been learned, sing *a cappella.*

Teaching tips: The rhythm is somewhat tricky, hence, counting in twos (two eighth notes as one beat) and in threes (one-and-a-half beats) will be easiest to handle.

7, Ameni

*Author/*Composer: Unknown; transcr., David Dargie, b. 1938, South Africa; Setswana language

Background: David Dargie, a German connected with the Lumuko Institute in South Africa, transcribed the song.

Theme: The song is commonly used for purposes of greeting one another as a sign of peace.

Liturgical use: It may be sung at the passing of the peace in a worship service. Alternatively, it may be used before or after the benediction as the last song, bidding farewell and wishing one another well for the period of separation.

Performance and style: When performing the song, preferably *a cappella,* singers turn to the right and left on every other downbeat. As they greet one another it is important to face their partners and express joy. Pace yourself as you lead the group. Do not sing so rapidly that the basses cannot manage all of the notes in their part. They must carry the rhythm of the song. Tempo: quarter note = 72-78.

Teaching tips: First rehearse the bass part. Once it is clear and established, then rehearse the treble parts. Thereafter, bring everyone in together.

8, Amina lele / Amina amen

Author/Composer: Unknown; arr., Patrick Matsikenyiri, b. 1937, Zimbabwe; Eng. trans., Umadjela Ahundju, Democratic Republic of Congo

Background: This is a song which arises out of the celebrative spirit of the people of the Democratic Republic of Congo. No matter what their situation in life, they will give thanks and praise to God.

Theme: This is a song of praise and thanksgiving.

Liturgical use: It is very fitting to sing this song when gifts, tithes, and offerings are presented in a service of worship.

Performance and style: The song is to be performed in a call-and-response pattern. A strong leader is needed to set the tone of the song. The song should flow and not drag.

Instrumentation: Use the drum and *hosho* (shaker) for various rhythmic effects. Tempo: quarter note = 110-116.

Teaching tips: Have the congregation learn the response first, and sing it until it flows.

9, Bani ngyeti ba Yawe / Let us praise the Lord, Yaweh

Author/Composer: Alfred S. Bayiga Bayiga, b. 1937; original language: Mungaka; French trans., Bayiga Bayiga; Eng. trans., S T Kimbrough, Jr.; Shona trans., Patrick Matsikenyiri

Background: Mungaka is one of the numerous tribal languages of Cameroon, and Mr. Bayiga Bayiga has written many songs of the Christian faith in Mungaka and other languages.

Theme: The song is a setting for one of the most ancient ascriptions of praise: hallelujah. It praises God the Creator.

Liturgical use: The song may be sung with zest at the beginning of worship.

Performance and style: The leader may embellish over and above the other voices. The "Hallelujahs" are the highlight of the song. The song should drive forward so that each time one sings "Hallelujah" it is indeed the climax of the song. Sing with joy! Tempo: a quarter note = 78.

10, Bless the Lord, O my soul

Author/Composer: Timothy E. Kimbrough, b. 1957

Background: This paraphrase and musical setting of Psalm 103 was originally written as a theme song for Vacation Bible School at the Church of the Holy Family Episcopal, Chapel Hill, North Carolina. The children were first taught the chorus and then on each succeeding night of the week a new verse of the psalm. By the last night of Vacation Bible School the parents and children knew the song from beginning to end and were able to join together in praise, with great joy, at the closing Eucharist.

Theme: While the primary theological emphasis is praise, it also includes subtexts which touch on penitence, the pursuit of holiness, revelation, and the establishment of God's justice.

Liturgical use: This song may be used in place of Psalm 103 when so designated by the lectionary or the preacher. It also works well as a song of praise, for example, in place of the *Gloria in excelsis.*

Performance and style: Light and contemporary; tempo (*moderato*): quarter note = 108

Instrumentation: Use piano and guitar. Having a set of congas, bongos, or a tambourine will help the congregation begin to feel the rhythm.

Teaching tips: Begin by teaching only the chorus to the congregation. A soloist or a choir might sing the verses the first few times the song is presented to the congregation.

Reference: It is recorded on *Global Praise 2* (CD 1-012, GBGMusik), and on *Youth Mission Chorale: Asia Tour 2001* (CD 1-020, GBGMusik).

11, O for a thousand tongues to sing; *refrain*: Blessed be the name.

Author: Charles Wesley, b. 1708, d. 1788, Great Britain

Composer: Ralph E. Hudson, b. 1843, d. 1901, USA

Background: Hudson arranged this refrain from early nineteenth-century folk and camp-meeting sources for his *Songs for the Ransomed*, (Alliance, Ohio, 1887). J. M. Hunt in *The Evangel*, 1909, adapted and arranged Hudson's music in a call-and-response form with this text, using the words "Blessed be the name" as an "interrupting chorus."

This version includes lines one and three of three stanzas of Wesley's original text, which was composed to celebrate the first anniversary of his conversion, May 21, 1738. It was first published under the title, "For the Anniversary Day of One's Conversion" in *Hymns and Sacred Poems* (1740).

Theme: Praise of God, salvation from sin

Liturgical use: Opening of worship, praise song

Performance and style: It may be sung by choir, soloists, and congregation as a call to worship, with gospel-style keyboard accompaniment. Tempo: quarter note = 96.

Instrumentation: Keyboard

Reference: The text is published with a different tune in *EM* (2002).

12, Laudate Dominum / Sing praise, and bless the Lord

Text: Psalm 117:1

Composer: Jacques Berthier, b. 1923, d. 1994, France

Background: This setting of Psalm 117:1 is one of the many memorable rounds and choruses from the ecumenical community in Taizé, France, a village in eastern France near Cluny, Burgundy. Since its founding in 1940, the community has dedicated its efforts to the renewal of the devotional life of the Christian church through the rediscovery and composition of simple songs and rounds. The songs/hymns are sung worldwide in many languages—and as such are truly ecumenical and global.

Jacques Berthier, composer, accompanist, and recitalist, was born in 1923 and served many years as organist of Saint-Ignace in Paris.

Theme: Everyone is called to praise God.

Liturgical use: Use it as a call to worship or in a choir and congregation in a festival processional. It may be used as a *Gloria* in any worship service, especially on Epiphany.

Performance and style: This chorus should be sung with vigor at the suggested tempo: quarter note = 96, but do not rush. It may be sung a number of times, alternating between choir and congregation or other groupings of worshipers.

Instrumentation: Handbells may be used, playing the open fifths of the chords in each measure, for example:

> m. 1, A E
> 2, E B
> 3, A E
> 4, G D
> 5, C G
> 6, G D
> 7, A E
> 8, E B

2nd ending: A E, D A, E B, A E.

Teaching tips: Have the sopranos sing the melody so that everyone gets acquainted with it.

Reference: Alternate harmonizations and instrumental parts are available from the publisher, GIA Publications, Inc. See "Copyright Acknowledgments" pages for contact information. Recordings of the piece are available from GIA and Les Presses de Taizé.

13, Nyanyikanlah nyanyian baru bagi Allah / Sing the Lord a new song

Author: Tilly Lubis-Nainggolan, b. 1925, d. 2002, Indonesia

Composer: Unknown, traditional Batak melody, Toba, Indonesia

Background: Tilly Lubis-Nainggolan is a name that is inseparably linked to YAMUGER, a Protestant church music organization based in Jakarta that seeks to promote the development of indigenous song. *Note:* In the published score of *GP2* the second word "nyanjian" should be spelled "nyanyian."

Theme: Psalm 148, a call to praise

Liturgical use: Call to worship, World Communion Sunday

Performance and style: Movement—see instructions in the *GP2* songbook. Dynamics—the last two lines of each stanza are repeated: "Bersorak sorai bagin Rajamu!" Begin softly and build to the end. You may consider performing this antiphonally with two or more choirs. Tempo: quarter note = 88.

Instrumentation: Angklung, a set of Indonesian-tuned bamboo bars could be used, if available, or guitar strumming with some percussion instruments. See the second page of the published song for percussion suggestions.

Teaching tips:
   a. Learn the rhythmic pattern of the first four measures.
   b. If one is singing in Bahasa Indonesia, teach the last four measures, since the words are repeated. The congregation can easily sing them while a soloist or an ensemble sings the rest of the text.
   c. Do not set a tempo faster than is comfortable for the congregation to learn the song. It is far better to "drag" the song a little and enable the congregation to sing it with confidence.
   d. Remember that Bahasa Indonesia is an open-vowel language, rather similar to Italian. Thus, the vowels are pronounced as follows: "a" is "ah"; "e" is "air"; "i" is "ee"; "o" is "oh"; "u" is "oo."

Reference: It is recorded on *Youth Mission Chorale: Asia Tour 2001* (CD1-020, GBGMusik).

14, Se Guds lamm / Lamb of God

Author/Composer: Tomas Boström, b. 1953, Sweden
Background: "Lamb of God" is based on the classical *agnus dei* (John 1:29) of the liturgy when the worshippers prayerfully repeat these words three times.
Theme: The last sentence of the song reminds us that God has taken away our guilt and filled our hearts with love.
Liturgical use: It is appropriate at the appointed place in the liturgy of Holy Communion. The congregation may also sing it during the distribution of bread and wine.
Performance and style: It should be sung meditatively and rather slowly. Tempo: quarter note = 110.

15/16, Gospodi pomilui / Lord, have mercy

Author/Composer: Anonymous
Background: These are two excellent and well-known settings from traditional Russian Orthodox liturgical music.
Theme: The mercy of God; see Psalm 8:14.
Liturgical use: The *kyrie* is used at the appointed place in the service of

Holy Communion. It may be sung a few times, usually three, and may be used before and after a Scripture reading, as part of prayers, or in a call-and-response manner with prayers of the congregation. It may also be sung as the background, accompanying prayer by a worship leader.

Performance, style, and instrumentation: The setting is for SATB choir/congregation, preferably *a cappella,* but it may be sung with piano or organ accompaniment. The tempo is *andante:* quarter note = 80.

Teaching tips: In order to build the four parts, rehearse the pieces in the following manner: 1) hum the soprano part without words; 2) all sing the alto part only; 3) sing the alto and bass parts together; 4) sing the soprano, alto, and bass parts; 5) all sing the tenor part; 6) sing all parts.

17, Kyrie eleison / Lord, have mercy

Composer: Mary K. Jackson, b. 1935, USA

Background: This setting of the *kyrie eleison* was originally composed for use in the liturgy of the Eucharist.

Theme: It is a plea for God's mercy to be bestowed on the one who offers this prayer.

Liturgical use: It may be used for the *kyrie eleison* at its appropriate place in the Eucharistic liturgy. It may, however, be used as a prayer or prayer response in almost any liturgical setting.

Performance and style: It should be sung simply and prayerfully at an *andante* tempo. It may be accompanied or sung *a cappella.* Tempo: quarter note = 60.

18, Ouve, Deus de amor / Hear us, God of love

Author: Simei Monteiro, b. 1943, Brazil

Composer: Guaicuru people (disappeared in the twentieth century); adapt. and Eng. trans., Simei Monteiro

Background: The melody was found in a book about indigenous music in Brazil. It was a ritual song in the Guaicuru language. The text was conceived as a memorial for the Guaicuru people and of their crying out to God, cries still raised by indigenous people in Brazil, who are far from being recognized in their individualities and as nations. It is an attempt to bring the unique flavor of their music into worship.

Monteiro's adaptation is considerably shorter than the original.

Theme: The clamor of those without a voice is the main focus of the revival of this song. Through it we hear the outcry of native peoples who have been systematically ignored or obliterated. It resonates as a *de profundis:* "Hear us, God of love! Hear this our cry!"

Liturgical use: It may be used as a penitential song, as a remembrance of indigenous people (focus especially on this issue). It is very appropriate for ecumenical and interreligious services.

Performance and style: The performance needs to be creative, but do not overdo the slides. An indigenous singing style in the Americas allows for *portamento.* Although not indicated in the score, it is recommended that you continue singing the song in order to maintain the original repetitive style.

The rhythm must be emphasized by stressing the syllables of the words. The first beat is always *marcato.* Tempo: quarter note = 120. A "circle dance" (danced in a circle) or a "row dance" (danced in a row) may be improvised in a kind of broken rhythm marked mostly by the right foot and with the head.

Teaching tips: Keep it simple. Teach first the words. Don't give all the instructions at the same time. Introduce the "new things" gradually. An *ostinato* beat can help sustain throughout. Although a penitential song, it should be presented in a vital and refreshing manner.

19, Kyrie eleison / Lord, have mercy

Composer: Ellison Suri, Solomon Islands

Background: As a member of the worship committee, Mr. Suri composed this *kyrie* for the Eighth General Assembly of the World Council of

Churches held in Harare, Zimbabwe, 1998.

Theme: Prayer, a plea for mercy

Liturgical use: It may be used as a response to prayers of confession, petition, or supplication, and general use throughout the Christian year.

Performance and style: Four-part singing is the norm for this piece. Wide, open throat singing is characteristic of the Solomon Islands. Tempo: quarter note = ca. 80.

Instrumentation: A guitar may be used.

20, ¡Gracias, Señor! / We give you thanks

Author/Composer: Jorge A. Lockward, b. 1965, Dominican Republic

Background: Born and raised in the Dominican Republic, Lockward currently lives in the United States and is Coordinator of the Global Praise Program of the General Board of Global Ministries of The United Methodist Church. This song of thanksgiving grew out of an effort to provide short, simple songs for liturgical use in the Spanish-language United Methodist Hymnal *Mil voces para celebrar* published in 1996.

Theme: This is a song of thanksgiving for God's people. The text of the song offers praise to God for who God is and for what God has done.

Liturgical use: It may be repeated as many times as necessary during the offertory and is also appropriate for use at any moment in the liturgy that calls for thanksgiving, such as the assurance of pardon, prayers of thanksgiving and petition, the end of the Eucharist, and after the benediction.

Performance and style: Depending on the context, this song may be interpreted in a range of tempi that may go from a slow, soulful quarter note = 66 to an upbeat quarter note = 96. This song has a built-in *crescendo* that starts in the fifth measure. Consider a gradual slowing down leading to a *fermata* on the second half of the eighth measure, realized by an emphatic rendering of the last two measures on the final repetition.

    The purpose of the sub-dominant (Eb) harmonic opening of the song is to create a sense of inevitability for repetition when the instrumentalists turn the final tonic chord (Bb) into a dominant (Bb7) on the second half of the last measure, leading back to the opening sub-dominant (Eb) chord.

Instrumentation: Organ, keyboards, guitar, trap set, and melodic instruments such as strings, flute/recorder, and brass may be used. If the song is to be repeated more than two times, consider building up the instrumentation to a grand finale in the last repetition.

Teaching tips: The sequential nature of its melody makes this song very easy to teach. A single rendering of the song by the song leader or the choir should suffice in most settings. One way to give a taste of the Spanish original to non-Spanish speaking congregations is to teach them the first two words (*Gracias, Señor*), which are repeated three times in the song, and sing the rest of the song in translation.

Reference: For more performance notes on this song, see the companion
book to *Sing a New Creation* published by Faith Alive Christian
Resources, 2850 Kalamazoo Ave. SE, Grand Rapids, MI 49560;
tel. 1-800 968-7221.

21, Holy, Holy, Holy: Sanctus from a groaning creation

Author/Composer: Per Harling, b. 1948, Sweden

Background: "Holy, holy, holy" is the final song in a musical, *Träd fram*,
by Per Harling about the tree of life, a passion allegory in which the
gardener plants himself and grows into a tree. This tree of life becomes
a playful friend to Adam and Eve, but in time it is polluted and dies
due to the greed of humankind; but then the tree is resurrected and
starts to grow again.

Theme: The tree metaphor is deeply rooted in biblical imagery, beginning
with the tree of life in Genesis 2. There are many other tree stories and
references to trees in the Old Testament. Jesus also speaks of himself
as the vine and the disciples as the branches. In the last book of the
Bible, the Revelation of St. John, there is again the image
of the tree of life: "the leaves of the tree are for the healing of the
nations" (Revelation 22:2).

The essence of the musical is that God's holiness, healing,
wholeness, and our human holistic perspectives go together. This song
from the musical is—like the ancient *sanctus* itself—a *credo* to the
holy and healing God. It is sung together with the whole groaning
creation, as referenced in Romans 8:18-30.

Liturgical use: The song may be used as the main *sanctus* in the Eucharist
service, or may be sung as a hymn in a service where environmental
issues are a concern.

Performance, style, and instrumentation: The first part of the song should
be sung in a traditional hymn style, preferably with organ, while the
second part, where the rhythm changes to a faster tempo, guitars,
piano, and other kinds of rhythm instruments may take over the
accompaniment. The song has a simple choral setting, but the whole
congregation should be encouraged to sing along, especially in the
first part, while the choir may sing the last part. Tempo: quarter note =
116.

22, Holy, holy, holy

Text: Isaiah 6:3, Matthew 21:9

Composer: Timothy E. Kimbrough, b. 1957, USA

Background: This is the traditional text used for the *sanctus* in the liturgy of Holy Communion in western Christianity. It was composed for use in the liturgy of the Protestant Episcopal Church by the Rev. Timothy E. Kimbrough, rector of the Church of the Holy Family Episcopal in Chapel Hill, NC.

Theme: The text, based on Isaiah 6:3 and Matthew 21:9, has been used for centuries in the Eucharistic liturgies of Christian churches to express the awe and wonder with which one is filled in worship before the Creator. It combines the outburst of "holy, holy, holy" from the prophet Isaiah with the messianic hope of the New Testament and the praise of the angels at the birth of Christ.

Liturgical use: Eucharist/Holy Communion

Performance and style:
The musical and vocal style should be *molto legato.* Sing in a connected, flowing manner.

Instrumentation: keyboard, organ, guitar

23, Bari sot, bari sot, bari sot / Holy, holy, holy

Author/Composer: Sarin, Sam, b. 1940, Cambodia/Australia; Eng. text, S T Kimbrough, Jr., b. 1936, USA

Background and theme: This version of the *sanctus* embodies the spirit of Isaiah 6:3. It is a Khmer (Cambodian) melody composed by Sarin Sam, for use by Khmer-speaking Christians in Cambodia and elsewhere. Though written earlier, it was first included in the *Christian Hymn and Worship Book* (2001) published by the General Board of Global Ministries for the churches of the Methodist connection in Cambodia.

Liturgical use: Holy Communion

Performance and style: It should be sung energetically in unison.

Instrumentation: Generally, sing *a cappella,* however, a single lead instrument, such as a flute or recorder may be used.

24, Le lo le lo lay lo

Composer: William Loperena, b. 1935, d. 1996, Puerto Rico

Background and theme: This offering from Puerto Rico is a very lively arrangement of the *sanctus*. The expression "le lo le lo lay lo" may have come from a similar African expression meaning "today." Consequently, the song is a reminder that the acclamation of God's power and might ought not to be postponed but celebrated instantly.

Liturgical use: The *sanctus* is used during services of Holy Communion following the words: "Therefore with angels and archangels and with all the company of heaven, we join in the unending hymn of praise."

Performance and style: In performing it, effort should be made to arrive at a Latin rhythmic beat. Because of the call-and-response form of this song, it should not be difficult for congregations to sing both in Spanish and in English, provided that the cantor is himself or herself comfortable singing in both languages. Tempo: half note = 80.

Instrumentation: Suggested accompaniment—piano, guitar, bass guitar, marimba, congas, maracas, castanets.

Reference: It is recorded on the GBGMusik CDs *Caribbean Praise* (CD 1-001) and *Tenemos Esperanza* (CD 1-016); on the CD *Du bist der Atem meiner Lieder* (Verlag Singende Gemeinde, Wuppertal, Germany)—a choral arrangement (SATB) is available from the same German publisher.

25/26, Slava vovyeki Tsaryu / Glory to the God of creation

Author and Eng. trans.: Julia Garbuzova, b. 1972, Russia

Composer: Anonymous; Russian folk music

Background: It is an original Russian folk song. The famous Russian composer Alexander Borodin used this song in his opera *Prince Igor*.

Theme: Glorification of the Holy Trinity

Liturgical Use: It is appropriate for Trinitarian ascriptions of praise and thanksgiving in all worship services, e.g., after the reading of the Psalter, at the offertory presentation, during Holy Communion.

Performance and style: Sing the four-part setting for choir or congregation, preferably *a cappella*. It may also be performed with piano or organ. Begin *mezzo forte* and build to *forte* on the last stanza. Tempo is *andante:* quarter note = 68.

Teaching tips: Stanza 1: all sing soprano part in unison; stanza 2: women only in unison; stanza 3: men in unison; stanza 4: all four parts.

27, Our Father, who art in heaven

Composer: Karen Armstrong, b. 1964, Jamaica

Background: This arrangement of the Lord's Prayer comes from a talented, young Jamaican musician who, throughout her life, has made contributions to worship with spiritual songs composed on a variety of themes. Her interest lies in creating music that effectively communicates biblical events and themes for children and young people. This is the result of her career orientation as a teacher.

Theme: The Lord's Prayer—the Triune God's sovereignty, reign, and sustenance of creation

Liturgical use: Appropriate for those places in the liturgy where the Lord's Prayer is used. It may also be used as an anthem setting of the prayer for children, youth, and adults.

Performance and style: Although this piece has been popular as a choral work, here the prayer of Jesus is set in a lively Caribbean mode that congregations will enjoy. Tempo: quarter note = 112.

Instrumentation: This version of the Lord's Prayer should be accompanied by a cross-section of instruments, with the percussion ensuring a steady rhythmic beat. Suggested accompaniment: organ, synthesizer (trumpets, trombones, and saxophones may replace the synthesizer), guitar, bass guitar, drum set, wood blocks, other percussion instruments.

Teaching tips: The song is very effective when male and female voices are allocated specific sections to sing.

Reference: It is recorded on *Caribbean Praise* (CD 1-011, GBGMusik).

28, El cielo canta alegría / Heaven is singing for joy

Author/Composer: Pablo Sosa, b. 1933, Argentina

Background: The song was written in 1958 as a first attempt to compose an "authentic Argentine Christian song." The melody is based on a tonal (without half steps) pentatonic scale (F-G-A-C-D), a feature of folk music on the west coast of South America on the Pacific Ocean along the Andean mountains. The author became acquainted with this type of music as it is being sung and played presently by the descendants of the Incan Empire, whose vast territory contained the areas identified as northwestern Argentina, northern Chile, Bolivia, Peru, and Ecuador. The Incan Empire was founded in the twelfth century by Manco Cápac and treacherously conquered in the sixteenth century by the Spaniards, led by Francisco Pizarro (1478-1541).

The rhythmic structure of the song is that of a dance-song known in Argentina as *Carnavalito*, more properly called *Huayno* in the Quechua language still spoken by the Inca people. Because of its lively character, it is frequently used by Christian (Roman Catholic) native people in the Carnival festivals (*Mardi Gras*) just before the beginning of the Lenten season, hence the name *Carnavalito*.

The text has a very simple structure, making it easy to memorize, so that singers do not have to depend on the printed page. There is a threefold purpose in this: (1) to keep the song within the style of oral tradition to which most folk songs belong; (2) to make it accessible to illiterate or visually impaired people, as well as children under school age; (3) and to enable spontaneous participation.

Theme: The three stanzas describe God's action within us and the way we respond to it. First: the glory of God is revealed to us in our daily lives. Second: as a result, the love of God unites us, creates a community. Third: we commit ourselves to proclaim the "Señor," to make him known, and to evangelize through our own lives.

Liturgical use: It is best used around the proclamation of the gospel, i.e., after the words of assurance and forgiveness, at the entrance of the Word, after the reading of the gospel.

Performance and style: a) It should be lively, but not too fast. Tempo: quarter note = 80. b) Keep in mind the robust, rustic way of folk singing. Do not be afraid of even shouting when you reach the high F at the last "aleluya." Do not approach it the way you would in Handel's "Hallelujah"! Rather, imitate the sound you produce to encourage your favorite football team.

(c) It is important to keep the *carnavalito* rhythm (one 8th and two 16ths) steady all the way through the song, especially on the stringed instruments. The *bombo* (or whatever you have as percussion) will maintain it, but with some freedom of variation.

(d) This is a loud song. Let it be heard, if not at a league's distance, at least as far as the last pew in the church. But if you are using a microphone, be careful not to distort it.

(e) No particular movements are related to the *carnavalito* when you sing it. Just relax and let your body swing slightly. But when you dance it, its choreography is quite similar to the circular sacred dances you find in many cultures of the world. Try it.

f) Say something (not too much) about the socio-cultural background of the song, stressing the fact that it reflects the life of people who have lived under oppression for over five centuries, since the arrival of Europeans in the Americas. Then have the people clap the rhythm, accompanied only by the percussion. Let them experience the feeling of "togetherness" which comes through a strong, common, rhythmical pattern. On top of that, sing the lines (accompanied by the flutes) and have the people respond with the "aleluyas." Add the string instruments. The song is short. It's all right to sing it over again, and then perhaps "tra-la-la" the lines and sing only the "aleluyas." Tempo: quarter note = 76-84.

Instrumentation: The original instrumentation includes guitar and *charango* (a small folk string instrument) to play the chords following the rhythmic pattern (one 8th note and two 16ths), *quena* (a folk flute) and *sikus* (similar to Pan flute, but in a variety of sizes, from high soprano to deep bass) to play the melodic lines, and percussion (mostly a big deep drum—*bombo*—played with a mallet and a stick, called *legüero,* from *legua*, league, because it is supposed to be heard from that distance).

The song may be played on a piano or guitar (with or without percussion). You may substitute recorders for *quena* and *sikus*. Folk music is often adaptable to modern instruments resulting in a fusion with other musical styles (jazz, rock, classical, *tango*, etc., thus creating a new and very interesting kind of language.

Reference: It is recorded on *Éste es el Día: Canciones de Pablo Sosa*, a product of ISEDET (Buenos Aires, Argentine).

29, E toru nga mea / Believe in God's Word

Author/Composer: unknown, Aotearoa/New Zealand, trans., S T Kimbrough Jr., b. 1936, USA

Background: According to the Rev. John Murray of New Zealand this is a well-known "refrain" or response of the Maori people to a formal speech in support of the speaker. It was first introduced at the Eighth General Assembly of the World Council of Churches and became widely known.

Theme: The text is based on the last verse of 1 Corinthians 13: God's word of faith, hope, and love.

Liturgical use: It may be sung as a response to the sermon or the reading of Scripture. Christian year: general use, but it may also be used during Holy Communion, a Love Feast, or a marriage.

Performance and style: The singing style is open-throat singing. The hymn is sung as a canon between leader and chorus or between two groups. Gliding tones are important for the style, but do not exaggerate them; just use a slight glide. Tempo: dotted quarter note = ca. 52. Sing *a cappella.*

Teaching tips: No rehearsal is necessary; just sing and signal the congregation to follow after you. The language is easy to pronounce, hence it is better to sing in the original language.

30, Na Ioane Bapetiso / There was a man named John the Baptist

Author/Composer: The text is attributed to Jacob Maka, who was also the composer of the music, b. 1906, d. 1961, Hawaii, USA

Background: Jacob Maka was an early choir director of the Wai'oli Hui'ia Church in Hanalei, Hawaii. His granddaughter Naomi L. Yokotake remembers: "Our family members have learned to sing these songs from my grandfather and my mom, Marjorie Maka Yokotake, who succeeded him as Choir Director of Wai'oli Hui'ia Church. Later, musical notation for each composition was written and included in the Hawaiian hymnal, *Na Himeni* [*Hapipule Hawaii*]. This distinctive style of singing these hymns has been passed down through generations within the Maka Ohana (family) and the Wai'oli Hui'ia Church Choir."[1] This hymn is an original composition of Jacob Maka.

Theme: It describes the baptism of Jesus by John the Baptist in the River Jordan. The hymn is usually sung *a cappella* and, because of its brevity, it is often included in a medley of hymns, or combined with at least one other hymn or song.

Liturgical use: It is appropriate for baptisms and for related lectionary gospel readings.

Performance and style: As indicated by Ms. Yokotake, the hymn is usually sung *a cappella* and may be combined with other hymns, such as *GP2*, #74, "E Ke Akua Ola," also a composition of Jacob Maka.

Teaching tips: Rehearse the parts with keyboard, if available, but sing *a cappella.*

31, There was a man named Jonah

Author/Composer: George Mulrain, b. 1946, Trinidad and Tobago
Background: This arrangement of the story of Jonah resulted from the
    composer's sheer fascination with the Old Testament account and of
    how God dealt with the reluctant preacher. He found it a powerful
    parallel to how many of his peers were resisting the call to proclaim
    God's Word. The intention is to ensure that the music conforms to
    the calypso idiom, that is, with a chorus that encapsulates the central
    idea.
Theme: The message is the mandate of the call to preach, a good example
    of "narrative exegesis" through which the songwriter tells and
    interprets a biblical story.
Liturgical use: It is appropriate for services which stress the call to
    Christian vocation and witness; also for ordinations and consecrations.
Performance and style: Maintain a steady, lively calypso beat. The stanzas
    should be sung in a narrative style, perhaps by a soloist, with the con-
    gregation joining on the refrain.
Teaching tips: The repetitive "Jonah, Jonah, go an' preach" should make
    the song appealing to children. In teaching the song, begin with the
    chorus.
Instrumentation: Piano, guitar, bass guitar, steel pan, drum set

32, Your Word will be a lamp

Author/Composer: Unknown, Thamilz melody, Malaysia; Eng.
    paraphrase: I-to Loh, b. 1936, Taiwan, and the Rev. James Minchin
Background: This is a traditional Thamilz hymn sung by Tamil-speaking
    Christians in Malaysia. It was originally translated into English by
    Calvin Chelliah, the first graduate (in 1984) from the Asian Institute
    for Liturgy and Music in Manila, Philippines. Minchin is from

    Australia and has been a major contributor of paraphrases of the
    hymns in *Sound the Bamboo,* the hymnal published by the Christian
    Council of Asia in a revised edition, 2000, edited by I-to Loh.
Theme: God's Word is a lamp and light; it is the love of Christ, the Bread
    of Life, and joy.
Liturgical use: It is appropriate as a response after the reading of the Word

or the sermon, or after a commitment and dedication. It is for general use during the Christian year.

Performance, style, and instrumentation: A guitar may be used for accompaniment; notice the ornaments and glides, which are important features of Indian music. Tempo: quarter note = ca. 92.

Teaching tips: Try to teach the song without using the music and text. It may be easily learned by rote.

33, Tua Palavra é lâmpada / I know your Word is a lamp

Text: Psalm 119:105, adapt., Simei Monteiro, Brazil

Composer: Simei Monteiro, b. 1943

Background: The Latin American Christian communities have developed a celebration around the Word of God, the Bible. The composer has observed in many Roman Catholic masses the beautiful way the Bible is acclaimed through the singing of joyful songs and dancing. This song is an attempt to create a celebrative moment before the gospel reading. The text is a paraphrase of Psalm 119:105, and the music is based on an old African-Brazilian dance rhythm called *lundu.*

Theme: The Liturgy of the Word is not only a time of learning, but one of Celebration. Like the Lord's Supper, it has a festive character. The community meets around the Word to celebrate God's presence and receives the authority to read and interpret the Word of God. The community experiences the "acclamation of the Word" as a unique experience of anticipation and fruition of the Word of God, which is complemented in the celebration of the Eucharist.

Liturgical use: This song is about the reading of the Bible, particularly the gospels. It may be sung in prayer services or any other devotional service, either public or private, and other occasions, such as a confirmation service or in Vacation Bible Schools.

Performance and style: It is a congregational song. Sing it joyfully, keeping the rhythm. It should be repeated several times at first or sung between the Bible readings as a response to the Word. Maintain the basic rhythmic pattern, but be aware that the song allows for many rhythmical variations. Free improvisations on the accompaniment are appropriate, depending on the size and singing abilities of the congregation. If the congregation feels uncomfortable with the tempo, slow down. The most important thing is the joy of singing.

The song may be danced by the congregation or a small group as the Bible is carried in procession to the lectern, altar, or other place in the worship space. Tempo: quarter note = 92.

Instrumentation: Guitars, percussion, and piano

Teaching tips: Some congregations may find this rhythm difficult. Speaking the words in rhythm without the music may be helpful. It is also possible to teach the rhythmic pattern by clapping or simply singing "la la-la. . . ."

34, For everyone born

Author: Shirley Erena Murray, b. 1931, New Zealand

Composer: Per Harling, b. 1948, Sweden; harm., Carlton R. Young, b. 1926, USA

Background: Shirley Murray started to write hymn texts very late in life, overcoming a frustration with the kind of texts she used to sing in her own church. Now she has become one of the most appreciated hymn writers of our present time. She is consistently Christ-centered, earthbound, and people-focused in her texts.

Theme: This is a moving and strong text about our human task of being creators—together with the Creator—of justice, peace, and joy on the only earth we know, our common home. The "table" in the text could be the table of the Holy Communion, as well as the table of justice, to which all are invited no matter what their religion, gender, race, or age.

Liturgical use: The song may be used at Holy Communion or in a service focusing on justice/peace.

Performance and style: In Per Harling's musical setting of this song, the stanzas are in a minor key and intended to be more reflective, while the refrain shifts to a dance-like, joyful style in major. Justice work should be joyful! The song, especially the refrain, is in a Swedish folk music style, in which the rhythm is highlighted by stressing the first and the third beat in each measure. If you know people acquainted with Scandinavian folkdances you might ask them to dance the song, especially the refrain. Tempo: quarter note = 112.

Instrumentation: Keyboard, guitar, bass, percussion

35, In the singing (Invocation)

Author: Shirley Murray, b. 1931, New Zealand

Composer: Carlton R. Young, b. 1926, USA

Background: See #34. Murray is a prominent hymn writer who has been represented in US denominational hymnals beginning with the *Presbyterian Hymnal*, 1990. The text was composed in 1996 as a response for Holy Communion. Young wrote the setting as the result of a request from a composition seminar he was conducting that he should write something "simple." That evening the six-note diatonic melody set to five chords was composed, faxed to, and approved by the author. The song was sung two days later at the closing of the seminar.

Liturgical use: Holy Communion

Theme: The two-stanza text features memorable lines with Eucharistic gestures, "hands expectant, open"; biblical and liturgical metaphors, "in the question, in the answer"; invitation to Eucharist, "Do you intend to lead a new life?"; Jesus was known to the disciples "in the breaking of the bread," Lk. 24:25; and the surprising, poignant petition, Jesus Christ "be the wine of grace and bread of peace."

Performance and style: The choir, soloists, and the congregation may sing the stanzas as they approach the table, and the elements are distributed, with the congregation responding with the refrain. Tempo: half note = 48-52.

Instrumentation: Keyboard, guitar, bass

Reference: It is recorded on *New Beginnings: the Music of Carlton R. Young* (CD 1-018, GBGMusik).

36, Vamos todos al banquete / Let us go now to the banquet

Author/Composer: Guillermo Cuéllar, b. 1955, El Salvador

Background: This is the "entrance song" for the *Misa Popular Salvadoreña* (Salvadorean Popular Mass), written by composer Guillermo Cuéllar at the request of Archbishop Oscar Romero. The text for this song comes from homilies preached by Fr. Rutilio Grande, the first priest to be martyred in El Salvador during the 1970s repression. Fr. Rutilio's proclamation of a "table large enough for everyone," his example of organizing the peasants from the town of Aguilares, and the horror of his assassination had a profound effect on his friend, the young Archbishop Oscar Romero, who was in turn martyred in 1980.

Theme: This is an invitation to all people to join in the feast of God's open table. The invitation extended by God to the poor of the earth comes with the imperative that all who attend the feast must work for a world where justice prevails and where resources are equitably distributed so that "no one will lack for food."

Liturgical use: The primary liturgical use of this song is the introit to the Eucharist. It may also be used as a call to worship for any service. Consider singing different stanzas of the song at different times during the service: stanzas 1-2 for the entrance; stanza 3 for the Eucharist; and stanza 4 for the sending forth. It is recommended that the names of the neighborhoods that appear in the second stanza be substituted with names of local communities in the surrounding area of each particular congregation.

Performance and style: This is a joyful invitation to God's "Fiesta"; it should be sung at a brisk tempo: quarter note = ca. 108.

Instrumentation: Feel free to use any instruments that might add to the celebratory nature of the song. A trumpet doubling the melody might be particularly effective, as tambourines would be for the refrain.

Teaching tips: Given the extended nature of the text, at first have the congregation sing only the refrain, with soloists or the choir singing the stanzas. Once the song has become part of the congregation's repertoire, it may, of course, sing the whole song. To assist learning the song, have one or more melodic instruments (trumpet, flute, etc.) double the melody of the refrain.

Reference: Two recordings of this piece are available:
(1) *Tenemos Esperanza* (CD 1-016, GBGMusik)
(2) *El Salvador* (in *La Misa Popular Salvadoreña,* GIA Publications, Inc., (404 So. Mason Ave., Chicago, IL 60638; tel. 800-442-1358)

37, We gather 'round your table

Author/Composer: George Mulrain, b. 1946, Trinidad and Tobago

Background and theme: This Eucharistic hymn expresses the composer's understanding that the bread and wine affirm the *real presence* of Christ at the table.

Liturgical use: It may be sung as communicants come to the table of the Lord to receive the bread and wine. Members of the group/ congregation may be invited to share what the sacrament of Holy Communion means to them. The first stanza may be sung or spoken as a grace before meals.

Performance and style: The hymn should be sung in unison in a lively, rhythmic fashion with guitar. If presented by a choir, stanza 1 may be sung in unison, stanza 2 by the women with SA parts, stanza 3 by the men in unison, and stanza 4 in four parts or unison *a cappella*. The congregation could be invited to sing stanzas 5 and 6 in unison with the choir. Tempo: quarter note = 92.

Instrumentation: Suggested accompaniment: piano, guitar, bass guitar, steel pan, drum set.

Teaching tips: Have a soloist or a choir sing the first stanza alone. The melody is very simple and the congregation should be able to join in singing on the second stanza.

38, I will receive the cup of salvation

Author/Composer: traditional Orthodox

Background: Originally this Holy Communion hymn for the Feast of *Theotokos* (Greek: mother of God) would have included a whole or most of a Psalm, sung throughout the communion of clergy and people. The verse that has survived was probably the refrain sung between other verses. This piece may represent an attempt to revive that practice.

Theme: The primary theme is that of Psalm 116, namely, the importance of calling on the name of the Lord who hears one's supplications. This is the God one loves for eternity.

Liturgical use: This psalm is used by the Orthodox as one of the prayers of preparation for the reception of Holy Communion.

Performance and style: In current use, this hymn is a verse (almost always from a psalm) that is chanted on one note immediately before communion. It follows the exclamation "Holy things for the holy," which is the ancient invitation to Holy Communion. It is followed by "alleluia" sung three times. It may also be sung repeatedly to a melody, as here, during the communion, with "alleluia" sung at the conclusion. It is sung *a cappella*.

39, Happy the one to whom 'tis given

Author: Charles Wesley, b. 1707, d. 1788, Great Britain

Composer: Thomas Tallis, b. ca. 1505, d. 1585, Great Britain

Background: Luke 14:15. This one-stanza hymn text appeared in the John and Charles Wesley's volume, *Hymns on the Lord's Supper,* which was published in 1745. The popular tune of Thomas Tallis, known as TALLIS CANON, has been used as a setting for many texts written in 88.88 meter.

Theme: Two central themes of the Eucharist are highlighted by Wesley here: Holy Communion is a feast of happiness and a feast of love, both of which are centered in Christ. The experience of God's love in forgiveness is already the experience of eschatological salvation.

Liturgical use: Holy Communion. This is an excellent hymn of preparation for coming to the table of the Lord. It is also appropriate for communicants to sing as they approach the table to receive the elements of bread and wine. It may also be used as a table grace.

Performance and style: The hymn should be performed *a cappella* and is intended to be sung as a four-part canon with an "open end." But every part can add half notes at the concluding "Amen" till the last part comes to its "Amen." Hence, the canon ends in unison. Take the canon in fluent halves, at first in unison. Each part sings it only once. Maintain a moderate tempo and do not drag. Sing with a sense of contemplative joy.

Teaching tips: Have a keyboard (organ, piano, other) play the melody all the way through. If a choir is available, have it sing the melody. Then invite the congregation to sing the hymn. The hymn may be sung as a four-group canon, with each group starting at the designated circled number (1-4).

40, The loaf of bread he broke

Author: Ephrem the Syrian, b. beginning of the 4th century, Nisibis, Syria
Composer and textual adapt.: S T Kimbrough, Jr., b. 1936, USA

Background: Ephrem was one of the foremost writers in the Syriac tradition of Christianity, and many of his hymns have been incorporated into the liturgies of the Christian church in both East and West. While his hymns are known more in the Eastern churches, some of them have been transcribed and adapted in Western hymnic and metrical forms and have appeared in hymnals of the West. The Episcopal priest, the late Rev. F. Bland Tucker, successfully adapted Ephrem the Syrian texts to metrical, hymnic style.

Theme: Ephrem strongly emphasized a theology of the presence of God, most assuredly in the holiest of all meals, the Eucharist or Holy Communion. This meal, which God has prepared for all humankind, is a mystery and a divine gift for all.

Liturgical use: Holy Communion

Performance and style: Sing it unaccompanied as a canon or round, as communicants come to the table of the Lord to receive the elements of Holy Communion. Tempo: quarter note = ca. 82.

41, Arriba los corazones / Come, praise God, all hearts together

Author/Composer: Néstor Jaén, b. 1935, Panama

Background and theme: The text is inspired by the ancient Latin words, *sursum corda* (lift up your hearts), from the mass. Around this text, Father Jaén, a Jesuit priest who is very involved in issues of social justice in Panama, has composed a Eucharistic hymn that invites all to find the bread and water of life in Jesus Christ.

Liturgical use: The primary liturgical use of this song is for the Eucharist, but it may also be used as a general call to worship.

Consider having a single dancer bring a loaf of bread, or a group of dancers bring the communion elements (and possibly the altar paraments) forward to the sounds of this song, either at the start of the service or before the Eucharist. Make sure the dancers are visible to the congregation and that they interact with everyone displaying the elements (and paraments) they are carrying.

Performance and style: This song is written in the *tamborito* style of Panama. It should be sung in a lively, rhythmic manner to a tempo of a quarter note = ca. 88.

Instrumentation: Keyboard, guitar, bass, percussion instruments

Teaching tips: A very effective way of introducing this song is to teach the congregation only the refrain and the response ("Come, O Lord!"), while assigning the stanzas to a soloist or group. The Spanish text for the response ("¡Ven Señor!") can be easily taught to provide a flavor of the original language. This response can be taught and sung in three parts.

42, Jeder braucht Brot / Lord, we need bread

Author: Hartmut Handt, b. 1940, Germany

Composer: David Plüss, b. 1957, Switzerland

Background: The origin of this song is actually stanza 2. It was originally written as a prayer before a meal. In its three-stanza form, it deals with the essential human needs of eating and drinking, of communication and hope transcending earthly life. David Plüss describes the background: "As we were looking for a liturgical hymn for the next Holy Communion service in the congregation of which I am a member, I came across a four-line text of Hartmut Handt. It was originally conceived as a spoken text for a grace before meals; however, I set it readily to a melody that is easy to learn. The melody builds with a description of our needs at Holy Communion and comes back to the theme with the final notes of the melody. As the hymn became an essential part of our celebration of Holy Communion, I asked the author to write some additional stanzas. The result is the hymn in its present form."

Theme: Jesus can indeed meet the essential needs of human beings, and this is experienced in the act of Holy Communion.

Liturgical use: Holy Communion or as a grace before meals

Performance and style: It may be sung *a cappella* or with instruments (*colla parte*), perhaps starting in unison (stanza 1), in two parts (soprano and bass: stanza 2), then in four parts (stanza 3). Tempo: quarter note = 72-78.

Reference: It is recorded on: *Global Praise 2* (CD 1-012, GBGMusik), and on *Du bist der Atem meiner Lieder 2 (*Anker Musik, Stuttgart, Germany). A German-language arrangement for four-part choir (SATB) and keyboard is published by the Christian Singers' Association (*Christlicher Sängerbund,* Germany). It appears in *EM* (2002).

43, Whose child is this?

Author/Composer: S T Kimbrough, Jr., b. 1936, USA

Composer: Timothy E. Kimbrough, b. 1957, USA

Background: The theme of the Global Gathering III (Kansas City, Missouri) of the General Board of Global Ministries of The United Methodist Church in 1999 was "Whose Child Is This?" This song text was written on the theme of this event and used in the program book. The first line recalls the Christmas carol, "What child is this?" But this song is about all children and had a unique origin. S T Kimbrough, Jr., attended a worship service in an Episcopal Church in the USA on a Sunday before he departed for England. During that service, a hymn by F. Bland Tucker with the unusual metrical structure of 6.6.6.6.888

was sung. After he arrived in London, he took a train north to York. The train car in which he was riding had a defective wheel and when the train would reach a certain cruising speed, the wheel seemed to echo the rhythm of the above-mentioned meter. As Kimbrough sat haunted by the rhythm, he began to write the text of this song. The tune was composed later by Kimbrough and his son, Timothy E. Kimbrough, who is Rector of the Church of the Holy Family Episcopal in Chapel Hill, North Carolina.

Theme: The song summons everyone to acknowledge that all children of the world are God's children and hence are the children of all peoples as well. These are the children we have known and not known; they are the suffering, sick, marginalized children, and those from wealthy families. They are the children of all races who suffer from racism. If we would be like Jesus, who said, "Let the children come to me," then we must open our arms to all the children of the world.

Liturgical use: baptism, general services

Performance and style: Sing in a flowing, ballad-like manner. Tempo: quarter note = 88.

Instrumentation: Keyboard, guitar, and rhythm instruments may be used; if drum set is included, use brushes only.

Teaching tips: Have the choir (perhaps children's choir) or soloist sing the stanzas, and then the congregation joins in singing the refrain.

Reference: It is recorded on *Global Praise 2* (CD 1-012, GBGMusik).

44, Mä silmät luon ylös / I lift my eyes to you, God

Author: Johan Ludwig Runeberg, b. 1804, d. 1877, Finland; trans., Per Harling, b. 1948, Sweden

Composer: Rudolf Lagi, b. 1823, d. 1868, Finland; harm., Carlton R Young, b. 1926, USA

Background and theme: In Scandinavia, Sweden and Finland have had many and important ties throughout history, even though the cultures are quite different. As regards language, Sweden, Norway, Denmark, and even Iceland to some extent, may understand each other (though at times with great difficulty). But with Finland it is different. The Finnish people speak a totally different language. Finland, however, has two official languages: Finnish and Swedish. There are also many Finnish-speaking people living in Sweden today. The author of the Finnish song "Mä silmät luon ylös," Johan Ludwig Runeberg, is a very well-known author in Finland, even though he has written mainly in Swedish.

This hymn for children, which originally was written in Swedish, is popular in Sweden (though with a different tune), but has never been connected with baptism in the Swedish church setting. In Finland, however, the Finnish translation of this hymn with its genuine Finnish melody has become *the* baptism hymn. No baptism can take place in Finland without singing "Mä silmät luon ylös."

Liturgical use: The song is appropriate for baptism but also for any worship service which stresses what it means to be a child of God.

Performance, style, and instrumentation: It may be sung in unison or in the SAB arrangement (except for two measures of the last line where there is a division of parts in the bass clef) as in the *GP2* songbook with organ or piano accompaniment. Tempo: dotted half note = 48.

45, I lift up my eyes to the hills

Text: Psalm 121 textual adapt., Jusuf Kamadjadja and S T Kimbrough, Jr., b. 1936, USA

Composer: Jusuf Kamadjadja, b. 1961, Indonesia; arr., Timothy E. Kimbrough, b. 1957, USA

Background: Jusuf Kamadjadja, an Indonesian of Chinese origin, received his church music training from the Singapore Bible College. He has served the Wesley Methodist Church, Singapore, since 1993 as Lay Ministry Staff for Worship and Music. He composed this setting of Psalm 121 for use in worship at Wesley Methodist Church.

Theme: Psalm 121, assurance of God's aid and sustenance

Liturgical use: It may be used as a prayer hymn or as the appointed psalm of the day. It is appropriate for Lent and all times of crisis.

Performance and style: This song reflects the current trend of church music in most Asian countries where western harmonic organization and style remain a strong influence. Yet one senses in it a plaintiveness and simplicity commonly thought of as Asian.

The rhythm should be flowing and easy. Do not interpret the direction of pitches to a higher range as an approach to the dynamic climax of the song. To the contrary, the range of dynamics in the song has a very narrow margin.

Instrumentation: Optional *obbligato* instruments such as guitar, flute, or violin may be used.

Teaching tips: To enter into the spirit of the song, invite the singers first to hum the melody softly without the accompaniment. Next, introduce the accompaniment with the humming while reading the text aloud. Finally, sing the song as written.

Reference: It is recorded on *Faith•Hope•Love* (CD 1-013, GBGMusik).

46, I will bless the Lord

Text: Psalm 34;1-5, 8-9, 14

Composer: Timothy E. Kimbrough, b. 1957, USA

Background: It was composed for use as a responsorial psalm in the Eucharistic assembly.

Theme: Its primary theme is praise.

Liturgical use: Psalm 34 is among those Psalms that may be sung at the Great Vigil of Easter in response to the lessons rehearsing God's saving grace.

Performance and style: This psalm setting is written after the style of many Taizé community psalm responses. It should not be sung too fast. Ideally a cantor or choir should sing the stanzas with the entire congregation joining on the chorus.

Instrumentation: This setting lends itself to a variety of instrumentations from organ and choir to piano/guitar and a small vocal group.

Teaching tips: Introduce the melody with a lead instrument, such as a flute. If time permits prior to the service, the leader may briefly rehearse the congregation on the chorus.

47/48, O choro pode durar / My weeping and my deep sorrow

Author: Simei Monteiro, based on Psalm 30

Composer: Simei Monteiro, b. 1943, Brazil; Eng. trans., Simei Monteiro

Background: The *baião* is a rhythm from northeast Brazil, one of the poorest and driest regions of the country. It is sung and danced in popular festivals. The mixture of two different styles and rhythms is intentional to express this ambiguity.

Theme: That one should be faithful in God's action is the central idea of Psalm 30. This central idea, expressed in the refrain, is present in many Latin American songs of hope, which celebrate the transforming presence of God and witness to God's actions.

Liturgical use: This song has multiple uses: psalmody, intercessions, praises for deliverance, healing service, and general use. Although personal, it may be used in communal services as a song of hope in times of trial.

Performance and style: There are two styles: the *baião* (dance) and the recitative (solo part). They are very different from each another, like weeping and laughing. The stanzas are sung freely as the recitative style requires. The refrain must be at the following tempo: quarter note = 110. Feel free to dance the *baião,* raising your hands at the refrain.

Instrumentation: Originally the *baião* featured *pífano flutes;* however, since 1940, the typical instrumental ensemble consists of an accordion, *zabumba* (wide bass drum), and triangle. If an accordion is not available, use an accordion sound on a synthesizer. A floor tom or another large bass drum may be substituted for the *zabumba.* The *zabumba* is played with a mallet on one side, producing an open bass tone, and with a stick on the other side, producing a higher pitched tone. The stick is also played against the rim, resulting in a syncopated 2/4 rhythm.

Teaching tips: First teach the refrain without percussion and then with accompaniment. Let the stanzas be sung freely in a recitative style by the soloist or group but avoid a dramatic or rigid performance. The stanzas should sound like a prayer.

Reference: It is recorded on *Tenemos Esperanza* (CD 1-016, GBGMusik).

49, Se och smaka Herrens godhet / Taste and see how good God is

Text: Psalm 34:8, Eng. adapt., S T Kimbrough, Jr., b. 1936, USA

Composer: Tomas Boström, b. 1953, Sweden

Background: "Taste and see" is an *offertorium* from the mass *Ett bord för mig* ("A Table for Me") that Tomas Boström composed in 1994, based on lyrics from the Psalter.

Theme: The theme is from Psalm 34, namely, that those who take refuge in God will be happy and will taste how good God truly is.

Liturgical use: "Taste and see" is a song for the liturgy of the table, Holy Communion, but it can also be used as a response to the scriptural readings during worship or as a song of praise.

Performance and style: One may feel free to use different percussion instruments, with influences from Latin America in the rhythm. As the table is prepared for Holy Communion, sing energetically and with movement. Tempo: dotted quarter note = 69.

Instrumentation: Guitar and rhythm instruments are appropriate for the lively performance of the song.

Reference: A choral arrangement is published by Verlag Singende Gemeinde (Wuppertal, Germany).

50, Search me, O God

Text: Psalm 139:23-24

Composer: I-to Loh, b. 1936, Taiwan

Background: This setting of the psalm text was composed as a prayer during a retreat at the Pacific School of Religion, San Francisco, California, in 1990.

Theme: Confession of sins, prayers for guidance

Liturgical use: It may be used as a prayer response before and/or after each confession and is appropriate throughout the Christian year.

Performance and style: It may be accompanied with broken chords, played on a guitar. The seemingly "wrong" chords are intentional —creating tensions and conflicts between willingness and unwillingness to confess guilt. Tempo: quarter note = ca. 80.

Instrumentation: Guitar

Teaching tips: Practice the large skips of a fifth. Avoid an accent on the higher tone; simply raise the voice lightly.

51, Khaw hai kham pha wa na / Let my prayer rise

Author/Composer: Solot Kuptarat, b. 1957, Thailand; transcr. and trans., I-to Loh, b. 1936, Taiwan

Background: This setting of Psalm 141:2 was taught by participants of a conference in Chiengmai, Thailand.

Theme: Prayer (offering of sacrifice)

Liturgical use: Use as a prayer of praise, thanksgiving, petition, and/or supplication. Christian year: general use. It is, of course, for Morning Prayer but one may change "morning sacrifice" to "evening sacrifice" for Evening Prayer.

Performance and style: The triple time is only for convenience of notation. Sing it through without stressing the first beats. Tempo:

quarter note = ca.76. Sing *a cappella.*

52, Halleluja! Prisa Herren, min själ! / Halleluja! Praise the Lord, O my soul!

Text: Based on Psalm 146:1-2; Eng. adapt., S T Kimbrough, Jr., b. 1936, USA

Composer: Tomas Boström, b. 1953, Sweden

Background: This "Halleluja" is from the mass *Ett bord för mig* ("A Table for Me," see song #49).

Theme: Praise of God

Liturgical use: It may be sung as a response to the gospel reading, as a hymn of praise to God, or as the appointed psalm from the lectionary.

Performance and style: The rhythmic expression is similar to a *bossa nova* style. Do not drag but rather sing it in a lively and forward-moving fashion. Keep it light and with crisp pronunciation of the words. Tempo: half note = 108.

Instrumentation: Keyboard, guitar, bass, percussion

Reference: It is recorded on *Global Praise 2* (CD 1-012).

53, Jesus in the morning (Give me Jesus)

Text/Music: African American Spiritual

Background: This is an example of the Christological focus of much African American worship; therefore, it can be concluded that "Jesus in the Morning" might have been created initially during a worship service. There is also reason to believe that it might have emerged during the nineteenth or early twentieth century. One reason for this is that its rhythmic drive lends itself to keyboard improvisations; thus, it is can be comfortably aligned with black gospel music because of the lilt, beat, and high energy.

Theme: Jesus, for the slave, was the closest link to Almighty God, the direct channel to omnipotent power. By virtue of his lowly birth, slaves could identify with and learn from him; he was equally accessible to the slave. This spiritual is a clear affirmation that Jesus makes himself available at any time, morning noon and night; therefore, he should be praised, loved, and served!

Liturgical use: This is a spiritual of praise and is appropriate at the beginning of the service, and especially as a morning hymn. Any song that focuses on Jesus, the second person of the Trinity, is appropriate at many places in an order of service. This song is especially appealing to children and youth.

Performance and style: It should be taught as a unison song, with parts introduced, as the group feels comfortable. It may be sung as a canon (or round) after the melody has become familiar. This is an excellent song in which to engage the entire congregation in signing (see *Teaching tips*) as they sing, as well. Key words in each stanza should continue throughout (e.g. *Jesus, praise him*, and *love him*), with additional concepts in each stanza introduced according to the ability of the group. Tempo: quarter note = ca. 69.

Instrumentation: Piano/other keyboards, organ

Teaching tips: This spiritual contains only eight bars and may be taught very easily and quickly by an energetic song leader. It may be taught *a cappella* or with accompaniment, with the added feature of vocal and instrumental modulation through the last two stanzas.

Reference: Evidence of the popularity of this song is the frequency with which it occurs in denominational hymnals, including the African American Catholic Hymnal, *Lead Me, Guide Me* (Chicago: G.I.A. Publications, 1987), where it is included in the Eucharistic section. The African American Episcopal Hymnal, *Lift Every Voice and Sing II* (New York: The Church Hymnal Corporation, 1993), includes this spiritual only in the section of hymns in reference to Jesus Christ. An excellent signing resource is Elaine Costello, *Religious Signing: The New Comprehensive Guide For All Faiths* (New York: Bantam Books, 1986).

54, Nú hverfur sol i haf / The sun sets in the sea

Author: E. Einarsson, b. 1911, Iceland

Composer: Torkel Sigurbjörnsson, b. 1938, Iceland; Eng. trans., Per Harling, b. 1948, Sweden

Background and theme: The Lutheran Church of Iceland, which is the main church in the country, recently produced a new hymnal (1997), where one may find this newly composed and beautiful evening hymn. Almost wherever one is in this small country in the far northern part of Europe, one is aware of the sea surrounding the island. Thus it is normal for all Icelanders to start with the words "the sun sets in the sea." In Scandinavia, however, original hymns from Iceland are rarely known. In the supplement to the Swedish hymnbook, *Psalmer i 90-talet*, which was published in 1994, this evening hymn was included, being the first Icelandic hymn ever in a Swedish hymn book.

Liturgical use: As the sun sets in the sea, "diminishing the light," this evening hymn is sung as a prayer for the whole world.

Performance and style: The hymn should be sung with reverence. Tempo: quarter note = 69.

Instrumentation: Keyboard, organ; it may effectively performed only with acoustical guitar.

55, Jesus Christ, the Gladdening Light

Author: Unknown; from The Greek Liturgy of the Hours
   Eng. trans., John A. McGuckin, b. 1952, UK
Composer: Carlton R. Young, b. 1926, USA
Background: Dr. McGuckin, Professor of Early Church History, Union Theological Seminary, New York, is formerly a Reader in Patristic and Byzantine Theology at the University of Leeds, England, and is a priest of the Romanian Orthodox Church. This lyrical translation of a third-century Greek "lighting" hymn is included in the author's *At the Lighting of the Lamps: Hymns from the Ancient Church* (1995, repr. 1997), one of seven books he has published.

   The *Phos Hilaron* ("Cheerful Light") is from the Greek Liturgy of the Hours and is a hymn of vespers. It dates from the third century and its author remains unknown. The ancient church from the second century marked the onset of evening as a time to give thanks to God. The central aspect of the earliest rites of Vespers was the bringing into the room or church of a lighted lamp to signify the resurrection of Christ—the "Cheerful Light" is the hymn that was sung as the lamp was carried in. Also, incense was offered to glorify God, and Psalm 103 was chanted. These three elements still lie at the heart of the Christian service of Vespers or Evening Prayer in many traditions.

   The chant setting by Carlton R. Young (see selection #35, *GP2*) was first sung during the Consultation on Orthodox and Wesleyan Spirituality, St. Vladimir's Theological Seminary, Crestwood, New York, January 10-15, 1999.

Theme: The central thrust of the hymn is the association of the symbol of light with the glory of Christ manifested in his world and in his church.

Liturgical use: The hymn originally marked the onset of evening, which in Byzantine times was regarded as the start of a new day, a time of resurrection and hope. The lighting of the lamp initiated the evening prayers of the church. As the lamp was carried into the synaxis, so the church proclaimed the resurrection of Christ and sang to the glory of God. Use as a gathering and processional hymn at the lighting of the candle at the beginning of evening prayer.

Performance and style: Originally it was probably chanted *a cappella.* Not much is known about third-century singing styles, but it was a communal hymn, and Basil the Great indicates in the fourth century that it was already regarded as very old and traditional. In the same century, Gregory of Nyssa mentions the death of his sister, who, though she was on her deathbed, instinctively turned when a servant brought in the lamp of evening and recited the prayer (*Phos Hilaron*) to mark the occasion. This suggests that the text and tune were probably widely known and sung. A C# drone may be added by male voices, organ, or an instrument.

Teaching tips: Byzantine chant was "pulsed" more than Gregorian chant.

Reference: It is recorded on *New Beginnings: The Music of Carlton R. Young* (CD 1-018, GBGM Musik). John A. McGuckin, *At the Lighting of the Lamps* (Morehouse Press, 1995).

56, Darkness now enfolds us

Author/Composer: Brother Paschal Jordan, O.S.B., b. 1944, Republic of Guyana

Background: Jordan, originally from Guyana, is a Roman Catholic monk who served for several years at the Abbey, Mount Saint Benedict, in Trinidad. Near Christmas of 1988, when the new monastery in Guyana was due to begin, he wrote this composition for the Benedictine monks while preparing the liturgy of the hours for the new foundation. The hymn was inspired by the story of Simeon, who, when he had seen the Christ child, asked that he be allowed to "depart in peace." Traditionally known as the *Nunc dimittis,* Simeon's words have been set in a variety of musical styles, from Gregorian chant to folk music.

Theme: May God's light at the close of the day lighten not only our lives individually but illuminate all creation.

Liturgical use: It is an ideal prayer to close an evening act of worship.

Performance and style: The hymn should be sung calmly and fairly slowly. Tempo: quarter note = 76.

Instrumentation: Keyboard, but acoustical guitar is very effective.

57, The food we now partake

Author/Composer: S T Kimbrough, Jr., b. 1936, USA

Background: The text is a table grace that was written at the same time as *GP2,* #40, "The loaf of bread he broke."

Theme: One gives thanks to God for food, for it is God's gift.

Liturgical use: It is intended for use by large or small groups before or after meals. It also appropriate for Holy Communion.

Performance and style: Sing *a cappella* as a canon or round. Tempo: quarter note = 112.

58, Be om fred / Pray for peace

Text: Traditional Irish prayer

Composer: Per Harling, b. 1948, Sweden

Background and theme: This traditional Celtic prayer with a musical setting by Per Harling articulates the necessity of peace as part of the whole human being—in body, mind, and spirit—in order for one to be open to God's peace. Or is it perhaps that by opening ourselves to the peace of God, we are able to let peace shape all our human perspectives and activities.

Liturgical use: This song is mainly used for the sending forth at the conclusion of worship. It may be repeated several times, while people depart from the place of worship. The song might also be used as the acclamation of the congregation in intercessory prayer.

Performance and style: Its character is reflective and Taizé-like. It should not be sung too fast. Tempo: quarter note = 76.

Instrumentation: Sing *a cappella* in parts. If needed, keyboard and acoustical guitar may be used.

59, Dievo Tėvo meilė / May God's love now bless you

Author: Original German text probably by Johannes Evangelista Gossner, b. 1773, d. 1858, Germany; trans., S T Kimbrough, Jr.

Composer: Johann Friedrich Francke, b. 1717, d. 1780, Germany

Background: Originally the song consisted of three stanzas. The biblical background is Deuteronomy 6:22-26. Gossner was a Roman Catholic, who later became a Protestant pastor, publisher, and founder of a missions organization. Francke was a Moravian theologian and church musician. It is a familiar benediction in Lithuania.

Theme: It is a prayer for God's blessing as one departs from worship.

Liturgical use: It may be used as a benediction at the conclusion of worship or as a gathering song of the faith community.

Performance, style, and instrumentation: The song may be sung in four parts or in unison with or without keyboard or organ accompaniment. Tempo: quarter note = 84.

60, Me yaco mai / Your kingdom come

Text: Matthew 6:10

Composer: Ilaitia Sevat Tuwere, b. 1940, Fiji; transcr. and Eng. trans., I-to Loh, b. 1936, Taiwan

Background: It was taught by a Fijian during a conference attended by I-to Loh.

Theme: The text is an excerpt from the Lord's Prayer (Matthew 6:10), namely, the petition that the Lord's kingdom will come on earth.

Liturgical use: Use as a response after prayers of supplication or intercession or after the sermon. Christian year: general use, Holy Communion, Advent.

Performance, style, and instrumentation: The Pacific islanders are famous for their light, natural, and open-throat singing, with basses singing the counter melody vigorously in their chest voice. This song is typical of this style of singing. The seemingly wrong notes or harmony, or the clashing of C and C# are intentional. Should this create too much tension, one might omit the C by singing an A. A guitar may be used or sing *a cappella.* Tempo: quarter note = c. 84.

Teaching tips: The "c" of the word *yaco* is pronounced like the "th" in the word "though," i.e., *yatho.* For the word *dai,* one should add an "n" sound before the "d," *ndai.*

61, May the love of the Lord / Wei yuan Shen di ai

Author: Maria Ling, b. 1961, Singapore

Composer: Swee-Hong Lim, b. 1963, Singapore

Background: The composer and author are husband and wife. This song was written originally as a lullaby for their first-born child, David. It was subsequently adapted as a blessing following a life-threatening incident.

Theme: God's love and care

Liturgical use: At the conclusion of worship; commissioning of missionaries or ordination

Performance and style: Keep the musical arrangement simple. It is possible to sing it without accompaniment. Tempo: quarter note = 84-96.

Instrumentation: Guitar accompaniment is possible with a recorder, flute, or oboe playing the melody.

Teaching tips: The music is composed in four-measure phrases with the third and fourth phrases being identical. One could introduce the tune by rehearsing in non-lexical syllables like "doo" or "lah."

62, Shalom

Author/Composer: Herbert Beuerle, b. 1911, d. 1994, Germany

Background: Beuerle composed this canon for a large group. It was sung for the first time at the 1983 German *Kirchentag* in Hannover by several thousand men and women. The *Kirchentag* is perhaps one of the largest meetings of Christians in the world. In May or June every two years, about 150,000 people gather from Wednesday evening until Sunday noon for Bible study, prayer, singing, discussion, and lectures on timely themes for Christians. Originally, the *Kirchentag* was a Protestant event, but the last one in Berlin (2003) was ecumenical. It was attended by around 200,000 persons.

Theme: The root "*slm*" is the basis of the interreligious words for "peace"—*shalom* and *salaam*—and herein lies its most significant meaning.

Liturgical use: This piece is particularly appropriate at the beginning and at the conclusion of a worship service. It could also be sung at the passing of the peace.

Performance and style: It should not be sung too rapidly, so that the effect of a bell-like sound can be developed. After it has been sung through one time, it can be immediately sung as a canon in multiple parts. If the leader gives a strong downbeat at each entrance of a group of singers, the multiple-part singing will be made easier. Tempo: quarter note = 72. Sing *a cappella.*

63, I wish God's love to be with you

Author/Composer: Unknown, Hong Kong; arr., Swee-Hong Lim, b. 1963,
Singapore
Background: The author and composer of this piece of music are not
known. This song is widely heard in Chinese churches in Malaysia,
Singapore, and Indonesia. Interestingly, translated lyrics (translators
remain unknown) in Bahasa, Melayu, and Tamil were subsequently
added and gained widespread popularity in churches where these
languages are used.
Theme: The invocation of God's blessing on those who depart
Liturgical use: Conclusion of worship, commissioning of missionaries,
ordination
Performance and style: This benediction is to be sung freely and quietly.
Tempo: quarter note = 108.
Instrumentation: Guitar accompaniment with a wind instrument (flute,
oboe, recorder) playing the melody is effective.
Teaching tips: The second and third phrases are identical. Introduce the
melody with an instrument while the group sings "doo" or "lah."
Teach the song at a brief rehearsal before the worship service.
Reference: It is recorded on *Youth Mission Chorale: Asia Tour 2001* (CD
1-020). A simple choral arrangement is available in the *GP Choral
Series* (CS 1010) and included on the *Anthem Sampler* recording.

64, Dieve, prašome Tavęs / Help us, God, we humbly plead

Author/Composer: Honoratas Owaldas, b. 1927, Lithuania; harm., Darius
Kudirka, b. 1969, Lithuania
Background and theme: Honoratas Owaldas was baptized in The
Methodist Church in Lithuania as a boy. He remembers attending the
last worship service in his home church in Kaunas, Lithuania, in June
of 1944, when the communists closed and confiscated the church. He
and two of his sisters, Antonina and Liongina, were three of the
remaining members of The Methodist Church who helped reorganize
Methodism as The United Methodist Church in Kaunas, Lithuania, in
August of 1995.

In 1998, after he was able once again to worship in the church of

101

his childhood, he wrote this moving prayer which calls on God to lead the people of Lithuania and other places away from evil, to deliver them from fear, and to sustain them by the divine presence throughout their lives. He lived through fifty years of Soviet occupation. During those years, he saw his church become a military storehouse, a cinema, a dance hall, and a sports club. The hymn is a prayer for God's constant presence, a plea that God will never abandon his people but guide them and grant them health and peace.

Liturgical use: One stanza or more may be used as a preface to intercessory prayer, or the hymn may be used for reflection and prayer. It is also appropriate for a watch-night service (New Year's Eve) or Easter Vigil.

Performance and style: Sing meditatively, but with conviction, in unison or in parts. It may be sung as a solo, with choir singing the SATB parts of the keyboard accompaniment. It may also be performed *a cappella* in this manner. Tempo: quarter note = 76.

Instrumentation: Organ, keyboard, or guitar may be used.

Teaching tips: Above all, encourage the congregation to sing prayerfully.

65/66/67, O Gospodi, sklonis ka mne / Almighty God, O hear my prayer

Author/Composer: Anonymous; traditional Russian folk music

Background: It is believed that this hymn was born in the 1920s, when Protestant Christians, like Orthodox Christians, suffered under the the communist regime in Russia. Many were imprisoned and killed. Hence, the music is filled with pathos and a sense of suffering.

Theme: This is a prayer that God will sustain believers in their gravest time of suffering and trial. See Psalms 11:4, 10:2, 15:1. God is the One who saves in times of trial.

Liturgical use: Liturgies of prayer, particularly for Lent and Good Friday

Performance, style, and teaching tips: The musical style is Russian folk music. It may be sung in unison or in four parts (SATB) with or without accompaniment. Sing stanzas 1 and 2 in unison. For variety, the women may sing stanza 1 and the men stanza 2. If a choir sings the hymn, it may hum a third stanza without words in four parts. On stanza 4, all sing (SATB). The tempo is *lento:* dotted quarter note = 60.

Instrumentation: May be sung *a cappella* in four parts or with piano or organ.

Reference: It is recorded on *Russian Praise* (CD 1-006, GBGMusik) and on *Global Praise 1* (CD 1-003, GBGMusik).

68, O Bozhe pravednuyi / O God, I come to you repenting

Author: Zoya Mesnyankina, b. 1948, Russia
Composer: Ludmila Garbuzova, b. 1948, Russia
Background: The text was written after the author heard a sermon based on Revelation 3:20 in 1996. It was the author's first step toward a relationship with God and a deep sense of repentance. Two Russian women have joined to create this moving hymn of repentance. Mesnyankina, a member of the First United Methodist Church in Moscow, wrote the text of the hymn, and Garbuzova, the pastor of the church and composer of many hymns and songs, wrote the musical setting.
Theme: God is merciful to all who repent and turn to God.
Liturgical use: This is a prayer of repentance and confession that is appropriate for daily devotion, Lent, and Holy Communion.
Performance style and instrumentation: Use as congregational hymn or with men's choir. Sing *a cappella* or with piano/organ. If sung by a choir, the order of performance could be as follows: stanza 1, men's choir; stanza 2, male or female solo with men's choir in the background with piano; the men's choir could sing a *kyrie eleison* as an interlude; then the second stanza could be repeated with an *accelerando con moto*. The tenors and basses could conclude with the *kyrie eleison*. The tempo is *andante:* quarter note = 76.

69/70, Blagodariu Tyebya, Khristos / For all whom you have saved

Author: "Gloria Group," Russia, written in the year 2000.
Composer: Ludmila Garbuzova, b. 1948, Russia
Background: This song was born during a seminar when the "Gloria Group," a planning committee of authors, composers, and musicians for the Russia United Methodist hymnal, *Mir Vam* (2002; see also *GP2,* #70), began its work on the outline of the hymnal. Ludmila Garbuzova, pastor of the First United Methodist Church in Moscow, was a member of the group.

Theme: The text is a prayer for peace and wholeness which Christ alone grants to all people.

Liturgical use: It is appropriate for the World Day of Prayer, Holy Communion, and ecumenical services.

Performance and style: It may be sung as a chorale with a solo or by the congregation. It should be performed with piano or organ. Begin softly (*piano*) and gradually build to *mezzo forte* and finally to *forte* on the last stanza. The tempo is *andante:* quarter note = 76.

Instrumentation: Appropriate instruments such as flute, violin, guitar, may be added.

Teaching tips: To familiarize the congregation with the simple melody, have a soloist or group of men and/or women first sing the entire hymn, followed by the congregation.

Reference: It is recorded on *Faith•Hope•Love* (CD 1-013, GBGMusik).

71, Ma na a e kai o Kalaupapa / On the blue waters of Kalaupapa

Author: Samuel Kauwalu, Hawaii (USA); Eng. para., S T Kimbrough, Jr., b. 1936, USA; trans., Dean T. Kauka, b. 1958, Hawaii (USA)

Composer: George McLane, Hawaii (USA); as sung by Mary Sing; arr., Ernest Kala, Hawaii (USA)

Background: Kalaupapa is an isolated community on the island of Moloka'i, site of a former leper colony. Though leprosy is no longer the reason for its existence, the community still flourishes. The song portrays people returning to Kalaupapa and remembering the place of their healing and redemption. Mary Sing was a patient at the leper colony and is the one who shared this song with others.

Theme: Sacred memory of healing and deliverance from a life of sin and sickness is cherished.

Liturgical use: Service of healing

Performance, style, and instrumentation: The song may be sung with organ or keyboard accompaniment, but four-part, *a cappella* singing would be preferable. Tempo: quarter note = 72.

72, Vai com Deus! / Go with God!

Author/Composer: Simei Monteiro, b. 1943, Brazil; Eng. trans., Simei Monteiro

Background: The text was written during a seminar on "Liturgy, Art and the City," Rio de Janeiro, Brazil (1999). It is part of a group of short songs, each dedicated to one of the seven (sometimes eight) canonical hours (the divine office). These hours of prayer, used for many centuries in the Roman Catholic monasteries, are also used as a *leitmotif* for different moods of the city according to the hours of the day. This song represents the second hour, *Laudes,* and depicts the city at 6:00 am. The text is inspired by the expression: *Vai com Deus!* (*Vaya con Dios!* in Spanish), which is normally said when someone is going out to work in the early morning. *Vai com Deus* (God be with you) is a way of saying "good-bye" to someone. Members of the family staying at home often say: *Vai com Deus!* It is also a kind of blessing. Considering the violence in big cities like Rio de Janeiro and São Paulo, one understands how powerful this saying can be, for it gives hope as one faces the dangers of the world.

Theme: God speaks to us through the words of our neighbors. God blesses us through tender gestures, a kiss, and the raised hands of parents and loved ones. There is also a domestic liturgy and as Christians we are dismissed every day and embraced in the faith and hope of our families. We are blessed by God to go out and to come in, not only in the church, but also in our private and public lives.

Liturgical use: It is a dismissal song, but it may also be sung in a farewell service or in affirmation of faith and hope during special services.

Performance and style: The *samba* rhythm should be maintained. Sing strictly but not in a rigid fashion. The *samba* rhythm allows some swing. It sometimes gives the impression that one is out of time. Therefore, the percussion must maintain a steady beat. The *samba* is easily danced in a simple two-beat pattern. It would be interesting to sing it while going out of the church or other worship space. Tempo: quarter note = 120.

Instrumentation: A guitar is better suited than a piano. Basic instruments are: tambourines, cowbells (*agogô*), floor tom (*bombo*), but maracas and other percussion instruments are also acceptable.

Teaching tips: Most people can learn *samba* melodies by listening to them played on a guitar or by using simple percussion.

73, Que Deus nos abençoe / May God bless us

Text: Numbers 6:24-26, adapt., Dagmar Borges, b. 1941, Brazil

Composer: Gelson Luíz, b. 1973, Brazil; Eng. trans., Simei Monteiro, b. 1943, Brazil

Background: This *tango* was composed in Rio de Janeiro, Brazil, during a seminar on "Liturgy, Art and the City," (1999). Borges has adapted the text from the biblical passage for Luíz's melody. It expresses a deep desire for peace to fill people's hearts, especially those living in the streets. It is a quiet, reflective blessing.

Theme: This is a blessing that is addressed to all people everywhere. Through the priesthood of all believers, the community is blessed.

Liturgical use: This song may be sung as a blessing at the end of a service or for a birthday celebration (persons, churches).

Performance and style: *Tango* singing uses *rubato,* which requires good communication between instrumentalists and singers. Pianists are encouraged to listen to the recording of the *tango* music of "Tenemos Esperanza" (*GP1,* #59, CD 1-016, GBGMusik). Emphasize the rhythm by singing while moving from place to place. Tempo: quarter note = 100.

Instrumentation: Use a *tango* group, if possible. Guitar, piano, or accordion *(bandoneón)*, and bass guitar are appropriate.

Teaching tips: Use the same observations for teaching *GP2*, #72, but remember that you are not asking people to perform a *tango* dance. You are the *tango*'s singers, though you may certainly feel free to move with the music.

Reference: Astor Piazola's works are recommended.

74, E ke Akua ola / O Lord of life, hear us

Author/Composer: The text is attributed to Jacob Kaoahi Maka, b. 1906, d. 1961, Hawaii, USA, but the music is Maka's original composition. Eng. para., S T Kimbrough, Jr., b. 1936, USA; trans., Dean T. Kauka, b. 1958, Hawaii, USA

Background: Jacob Maka was an early choir director of the Wai'oli Hui'ia Church in Hanalei, Hawaii. His granddaughter, Naomi L. Yokotake remembers: "Our family members have learned to sing these songs from my grandfather and my mom, Marjorie Maka Yokotake, who succeeded him as choir director of Wai'oli. Later, musical notation for each composition was written and included in the Hawaiian hymnal, *Na Himeni*. This distinctive style of singing these hymns has been passed down through generations within the Maka Ohana and the Wai'oli Hui'ia Church Choir Ohana [family]."[2]

This hymn was contributed by the Maka family in memory of their father, Jacob Maka, to the United Church of Christ Hawaiian hymnal, *Na Himeni Haipule Hawaii.*

Theme: The literal translation is: "God, please hear our prayer and help us."

Liturgical use: It may be used as a preface to prayer, but it is generally used as a prayer response during worship with or without accompaniment.

Performance, style, and instrumentation: It may be sung with organ or keyboard but four-part *a cappella* singing is preferred. Tempo: quarter note = 100.

75, Faafetai i le Atua / Thanks to God, author of living

Text/Music: Traditional Samoan hymn

Background: This traditional hymn is commonly used in Samoa as a hymn for gathering and an invitation to praise God. According to Rev. Etiuoti, the former principal of the Methodist seminary in Samoa, this hymn is also sung on national occasions such as the opening of the Samoan Parliament. Similar versions of this hymn (slight changes in melodic line) can be found in the hymnic repertoire of the Presbyterian and Congregational Churches in Samoa.

Theme: Thanksgiving

Liturgical use: Thanksgiving, harvest festival, intercessory prayer (stanza 3)

Performance and style: Call-and-response is a common musical practice of the Pacific Islands. This song is a rather western, stylized form of this musical style. Repeat the bass and tenor lines in an echo-like effect, and build to a double *forte* at the final "alleluia." Tempo: quarter note = 72.

Instrumentation: May be sung *a cappella* or with keyboard.

Teaching tips: Teach each vocal line separately and then sing in four parts.

76, Holy God, Holy Mighty

Author/Composer: Unknown

Background: (See the above explanation of *GP1*, #1, for the background of the Trisagion ["Thrice-Holy"]). Though the text is obviously based on Isaiah 6:3, its origin is not known. However, by the fifth century it was prominent in the Constantinople Liturgy and was mentioned at the Council of Chalcedon.

The text continues in popular usage in Orthodox liturgies, though the structure and style of its presentation have changed. In current Orthodox worship, the Trisagion has been separated from the psalm verses, yet it has retained a portion of its function as an introit hymn.

Theme: The hymn consists of two parts: (a) an affirmation or exclamation and (b) a prayer.

Liturgical use: The Trisagion is sung by the choir after the "Little Entrance" of the Divine Liturgy (the "Entrance" with the gospel). However, on feast days it is replaced with "As many as have been baptized into Christ . . ." Originally the "Little Entrance" accompanied the entry of the bishop into the church at the outset of the liturgy. The Trisagion was sung as the processional.

Elizabeth Theokritoff notes: "The Trisagion is also sung repeatedly (without 'Glory. . .' and the partial repetition) at the funeral procession and, notably, at the procession with the winding sheet of Christ on Holy Friday, whence it passed into the Roman and western rites (in Greek and Latin) as part of Holy Friday services. But on those occasions, a different melody would probably be used."[3]

Performance and style: It is sung *a cappella.*

77/78, Neeg nplajteb tau txais tshaav ntuj / God, our God, sends the rain

Author: Unknown

Composer: Sou Yang, Laos/USA

Background: This was probably a Lao hymn (though it cannot be established absolutely) that was translated into Hmong sometime in the 1950s and 1960s, when many Hmong first became Christians. It may have been a Hmong text at the outset, and the author used the Lao language for lyrics, since the written Hmong language had not been fully established at the time. It was used as a Christian hymn as early as the 1960s, but there was neither musical notation nor any accompaniment then; it was sung *a cappella.*

Theme: The text of the song views the rain which falls upon the earth as a blessing from God, the Owner/Creator of heaven and earth. The Hmong people, as well as almost all people in Southeast Asia, have only two seasons (tropical seasons): rainy and monsoon. Rain and sunshine are two important components of life on which people depend for crops and produce. This hymn expresses thanks to God, who created and provides sunshine and rain for people everywhere.

The hymn has three parts: the first stanza, which praises and glorifies God, stands alone; the second and third stanzas ask God for the blessings of power and strength to work, face tasks, and follow God's will; and the fourth stanza stresses the result and outcome of a life of endurance, perseverance, and persistence—blessed eternity with God.

The first stanza contrasts darkness and light, which occur daily in every part of the planet. The second and third stanzas ask for the blessings of a good name and integrity in doing God's work, that God will bless one's works during the year with fruitfulness, and that God's Holy Spirit will teach us to honor and please God. The last verse is about enduring hardship in this world.

Other themes that run through this song are: (a) God is in control and is the source of eternity; (b) sunshine bestows light; (c) life itself means eternity with God. The mandate to all is that we are to proclaim and share the Good News of salvation, God's mission, and eternal life; God is the source of power, light, and life for the world.

Liturgical use: Use as a hymn of praise. It is appropriate for Thanksgiving Day, New Year's Day, mission, evangelism, sharing of the gospel, devotion, and inspiration.

Performance, style, and instrumentation: The hymn was probably originally sung *a cappella,* but some groups have added keyboard and other instruments. It can be sung by two groups: men and women, adults and young people, leader and congregation/people. A suggested format for singing is: all sing the first stanza; men, adults, or leader the second stanza; others the third; and all the last stanza. Most of all, sing from the bottom of the heart to glorify God.

Teaching tips: Sing with or without instruments. Hum or sing the words in one large group or form small groups and repeat after one another.

References:
• *Hmong United Methodist Phoonkauj Qhuas Vaajtswv*, Hymn 273, The Hmong Christian Community United Methodist Church, first edition, 2003
• *Cov Ntseeg Yesxus Phoo Hu Nkauj*; Hymn 270, The Hmong Community United Methodist Church, St. Paul, Minnesota, 1986
• Cassette; Hmong Community UMC, St. Paul, Minnesota, 1988

79, Na o e ha ma ni tei e nei ao / O our God, you created this our world

Author/Composer: Unknown, Tahitian; transcr., trans., and author of stanzas 2 and 3: I-to Loh, b. 1936, Taiwan

Background: This song was taught by a Tahitian at a conference in Geneva, Switzerland.

Theme: God's love, stewardship of God's creation, ecology, offering

Liturgical use: It may be used as an offertory hymn, for stewardship commitment, and presentation of the elements at Holy Communion. Christian year: general, ecology Sunday, World Communion Sunday, Thanksgiving Day, Harvest Festival.

Performance and style: Sing without any accompaniment. Humming or "oo" is the congregation's expression of approval or agreement with the statement by the leader (soloist). The choir and/or congregation should sing in harmony as a symbol of unity or unanimous support/commitment. Tempo: quarter note = 60.

Teaching tips: Let the choir and the congregation practice the two chords first: GBD and DF#C. The call-and-response should tie together smoothly without any interruption.

80, Tian shang de fu qin da ci bei / Great are your mercies

Author: Chao Tzu-chén, b. 1888, d. 1979, China; English para., Frank W. Price

Composer: Unknown, Chinese folk song; arr., Bliss Wiant, b. 1895, d. 1975, USA

Theme: God's mercy and compassion

Liturgical use: Services of praise and thanksgiving, Lent

Performance and style: While the hymn is scored for four vocal parts, it should be sung in unison as was the original Chinese folk tune. Nevertheless, it is sometimes sung in four parts in China today. It should be sung in an easy and flowing manner. Tempo: quarter note = 76.

Instrumentation: Keyboard

Teaching tips: This through-composed hymn consists of several four-measure phrases. Teach the hymn by having the congregation repeat each phrase after the leader has sung it. The leader should avoid being overzealous in correcting wrong pitches or rhythm. As the congregation's confidence grows, it should be able to sing the hymn independently.

Reference: It is recorded on *Youth Mission Chorale: Asia Tour 2001* (CD 1-020, GBGMusik). A simple choral arrangement of this work is available in the *GP Choral Series* (CS 1016) and included on the accompanying CD, *Anthem Sampler*.

81, Come, thou everlasting Spirit

Author: Charles Wesley, b. 1707, d. 1788, Great Britain
Composer: Carlton R. Young, b. 1926, USA
Background and theme: This lyrical expression of the *epiclesis*, the Eucharistic prayer for the descent of the Holy Spirit, was included by Charles and John Wesley in #16 of *Hymns on the Lord's Supper*, 1745. Young included this setting of the Wesley text in his paper "A Survey of Eastern Sources in British and American Methodist Hymnals," presented at the consultation on "Orthodox and Wesleyan Spirituality," St. Vladimir's Orthodox Theological Seminary, Crestwood, New York, January 10-15, 1999. The tune is named WAINWRIGHT in recognition of the contributions to Eucharistic theology by Geoffrey Wainwright.
Liturgical use: It is appropriate for singing by a soloist, the choir, or congregation as the people partake of Holy Communion.
Performance and style: The hymn is intended to be sung in unison. It may be accompanied quietly on the organ, keyboard, or guitar. Tempo: quarter note = ca. 76.
Instrumentation: Guitar chords are included for optional guitar accompaniment.
Reference: It is recorded on *New Beginnings: The Music of Carlton R. Young* (CD 1-018, GBGMusik). See the facsimile reprint of the first edition of *Hymns on the Lord's Supper*, 1745 (Madison, NJ: The Charles Wesley Society, 1995). See Wainwright's preface to *Hymns on the Lord's Supper*, page ix, for commentary on this hymn. See also *Orthodox and Wesleyan Spirituality*, edited by S T Kimbrough, Jr. (Crestwood, NY: St. Vladimir's Seminary Press, 2002).

82, O Great Spirit

Author/composer: Unknown, Native American origin; transcr., Pablo

Sosa, b. 1933, Argentina;

Text/Music: as sung by McClellamin (1993),
adapted from a song by Nuxalk Young People, Canada

Background: This is one of the songs that Native Americans in
Canada brought to a workshop led by Pablo Sosa on Music and
Liturgy at the Vancouver School of Theology in 1993.

The resentment provoked by the plundering of their culture (as
by whites) makes it very difficult for native people to share their songs
with "strangers." Pablo Sosa was allowed to record and transcribe only
two songs on that occasion. This is one of them. The reason for the
permission was the fact that it is not actually an original native song,
but an adaptation. Sosa states: "Even if this could not be actually
documented, the fact is that we never did hear the song sung in any
original native language, but only in this English translation."

Theme: The very reason for the existence of religions is to see God! This
is the mystical desire of human beings throughout history. "Great
Spirit" is of course the way to speak of God in native North American
(US/Canada) religious language. With simple, direct words ("how I
long to hear your voice . . . to see your face . . . to touch your hand")
the song portrays the deepest need of human beings: a revelation of
their hidden Creator. "Away hey-ho . . ." is the sigh of the soul longing
for everything God is: a reason to live, an answer to our enigmas, hope
for the future, strength against fear.

Liturgical use: It makes a very effective call to worship or to prayer.

Performance and style: It should be sung slowly, but with a feeling of
binary rhythm (2/2, not 4/4). The song should be well vocalized and
sung very expressively. Use *glissandi* from one note to the next,
especially at the beginning. Sing it "freely"; do not stress the beat. Use
very soft percussion at the end. Use a very intense middle voice. Sing
each phrase and have people repeat after you.

There is no movement attached to the song, but it makes a very
fine piece of modern dance (if a good dancer is available). Tempo:
quarter note = 84.

Instrumentation: Use only a small drum.

83, Uyai mweya wakachena / Come now, come, O Holy Spirit

Author/Composer: Patrick Matsikenyiri, b. 1937, Zimbabwe

Background: The inspiration for this song comes from the frustration of the church throughout the world, not only in Zimbabwe, in realizing God's reign of justice and peace. Hence, one feels the need to call upon the Holy Spirit to come and instill hope in God's people. This is true of Old Testament prophets and of the New Testament disciples. The Holy Spirit has provided hope to the faithful in every period of history.

The author/composer has said this of the song's composition: "The night I composed this song, I felt tears dripping from my eyes as I thought of individuals I knew who had endured terrible experiences because of their determination to be faithful Christians. Hope alone in God's love saw them through those times and has seen me through such times as well."

Theme: The central theme is belief in the Holy Spirit. No matter what our circumstances in life, the Holy Spirit guides us in the right direction. The children given to us live in hope. Christians all over the world live in hope. People of faith have survived life-threatening moments and events through hope.

Liturgical use: The song has multiple uses: an invocation, before and after petitions in intercessory prayer, and the affirmation of a sermon on the power of the Holy Spirit.

Performance and style: Do not rush the song. It should be like showers of blessing falling on the congregation. The tempo should be very steady. The melody needs to be sung sweetly. The bass needs to be vibrant to solidify the song, while the rest of the parts blend to create the harmony. Go through the text first to ensure confidence.

Instrumentation: Use drums and *hosho* (shaker). The use of keyboard is optional, depending on the strength of the choir or congregation. When the congregation is not familiar with the language, the keyboard adds confidence. The people will follow and perhaps get into the spirit of the song better at first with the keyboard than without it. After the congregation has learned the melody well, sing the song *a cappella* but with rhythm instruments.

Reference: It is recorded by the Africa University Choir on *Africa Praise 1* (CD 1-004, GBGMusik).

84, All praise to our redeeming Lord

Author: Charles Wesley, b. 1707, d. 1788, Great Britain

Composer: Swee-Hong Lim, b. 1963, Singapore

Background: This setting and the one of "Ye Servants of God" (*GP2,* #116) by Swee-Hong Lim were created specifically with the intention of breathing new life into the poetical work of Charles Wesley, and thus to make his work musically accessible to a younger generation of Christians.

Theme: Church unity, formation of community, Christian fellowship

Liturgical Use: The hymn may be sung before the passing of the peace, on Human Relations Sunday, Church Unity Sunday, Week of Prayer for Christian Unity. It is excellent for the opening of worship.

Performance and style: The hymn should be sung in an upbeat and rhythmic manner. One should adopt the Caribbean calypso rhythm and its syncopation style, e.g., reggae. Tempo: quarter note = 120.

Instrumentation: A worship band of guitars, drums, and synthesizers would be appropriate. Additional percussion instruments, such as a triangle and percussion instruments of Afro-Caribbean origin, may be used. Use the musical score as a guide rather than the prescribed style of performance practice. Improvisation by the keyboard and other instruments is preferred.

Teaching tips: The melody is made up of two phrases consisting of four measures each. Have the people repeat each phrase after the leader, and the hymn will be learned very quickly.

85, Jesus, Lord, we look to thee

Author: Charles Wesley, b. 1707, d. 1788, Great Britain

Composer: Swee-Hong Lim, b. 1963, Singapore

Background: This hymn is part of a collection of five contemporary Asian hymn settings that the composer created for Chinese Methodist congregations in Asia: *Hymns in United Worship* (Hong Kong: World Federation of Chinese Methodist Churches, 1997).

Theme: Church unity, formation of community

Liturgical use: Epiphany, Human Relations Sunday, Church Unity Sunday

Performance and style: An attempt has been made to create a Chinese-style accompaniment. This can be realized only by strictly following the notated score. The music needs to be delicate rather than pulsating. Observe a regular four-measure phrase pattern. Tempo: quarter note = 84.

Instrumentation: Two types of accompaniment are possible: (a) the piano as notated; (b) a less formal setting on the piano or guitar using the notated chords.

Teaching tips: This is a through-composed hymn, brief and simple enough to be sung through once by the leader before the congregation joins in singing.

86, In the morning when I rise (Give me Jesus)

Author/Composer: Unknown, African American Spiritual

Background: This spiritual, also identified by the title, "Give me Jesus," is another of many examples of Christianized African American slaves' close identity with Jesus, not only as the author of the faith and source of salvation but as the closest friend one can have. Jesus is sympathetic and powerful and knows humankind's desire to wield power rather than act with sympathy.

Dr. Evelyn D. White, the arranger of this spiritual, distinguished herself as a choral director and arranger at Howard University, Washington, DC. In addition to a compilation of choral arrangements of spirituals and anthems by black composers, one of her arrangements is published in *Lift Every Voice and Sing II: An African America Hymnal* (New York: The Church Hymnal Corporation, 1993), page 123.

Theme: The spiritual is a statement of faith: When I rise in the morning, when I am experiencing "dark midnight," or when I am dying, I turn to Jesus for strength and help. (See additional perceptions in notes on "Jesus in the Morning," *GP2,* #53).

Liturgical use: Trinity Sunday, as a morning hymn

Performance and style: This spiritual is deeply emotional and should be sung slowly. Once the community gets a feel for the melodic line, it should be encouraged to sing in harmony. Tempo: quarter note = 86.

87, Sveikas, Jėzau gimusis / Jesus Child, we greet you

Text/Music: Traditional Lithuanian folk hymn

Background: This is one of the most traditional Lithuanian Christmas hymns. It reminds all to greet the infant Jesus and rejoice at his birth.

Theme: The Incarnation. This Christmas hymn exudes joy! It reflects the actualized joy of Emmanuel, "God with us."

Liturgical use: Advent and Christmas; it is an excellent hymn for children's worship and for a processional on Christmas Day and during Christmastide.

Performance and style: The hymn should be sung in a steady 4/4 tempo: quarter note = 88. Ask the people to convey the joy expressed in this hymn in their singing.

Instrumentation: The more instruments one can add, the better! A brass quartet would be particularly appropriate. Consider having a trumpet introduce the hymn by playing the melodic line through before the singing begins.

Teaching tips: Since the music of measures 1 and 2 of each stanza is repeated in measures 3 and 4, have a soloist or the choir line out measures 1 and 2 of stanza 1, which are thereafter repeated by the congregation. This same procedure may be followed for the refrain in which measures 1 and 2 are repeated musically by measures 3 and 4. The last five measures of the refrain should be lined out the first time through by the soloist or choir. Once this is completed with one stanza the congregation will easily sing stanzas 2 and 3.

88, Come, Lord Jesus

Author/Composer: Mary K. Jackson, b. 1935, USA

Background: The song was originally written as an anthem for the Sanctuary Choir at East Lake United Methodist Church in Birmingham, Alabama, and later transcribed as a hymn.

Theme: The text is a prayer for the coming of the Christ child as a light and a guide for all peoples, bring healing, love, joy, and hope.

Liturgical use: Though it was first used during the season of Advent, it may be effective as part of any liturgy that emphasizes the hope Christ brings to individuals and to the world.

Performance and style: The range of tempo indicated may be used at the discretion of the song leader. Unison or part-singing will be effective. Tempo: quarter note = 96-108.

Instrumentation: Piano, organ, or guitar accompaniments are acceptable.

89, Child of Wonder

Author/Composer: Sharon K. Cooper, b. 1946, USA

Background: The text is based on a prayer written by St. Francis of Assisi after a forty-day fast on Mount La Verna two years before his death in 1224. He composed the prayer and gave it, along with others, to his friend, Brother Leo. The original prayer on which the text of the song is based is found on page 14 in *Praying With St. Francis.*

Theme: The song is an expression of St. Francis's adoration of Jesus Christ, the one who unreservedly offers himself freely to God's creation. The descriptions of Jesus may sound a bit simplistic, but the substance of which the author speaks is very deep and rooted in his experience of the Unmanifested One. He comes to know Christ through his own contemplative and heart-practice in daily life. The God-self revealed in and through Christ is one of total Love and he is united in Love with all that "IS." Therefore, he moves through the totality of human experience with its extremities of rejection and joy. Christ is imbued completely with the Grace of a Presence. He *listens* and receives life as it is. St. Francis recognizes this as the height of beauty and that this is the One who brings true peace and justice to the world.

Liturgical use: It may be used on the first Sunday of Advent or any season. After a prayer of confession or before prayers of intercession, invite the congregation to a contemplative moment of brief silence. Name before the congregation situations in need of healing and restoration in the world, in the nation, in the local community, and in more intimate living situations. Invite all to a brief time of silence to gaze upon the Child of Wonder, or to say in silence to themselves the word "peace" or "shalom" in their own language, or to focus on the Breath which breathes the same air as every other creature on the planet.

Performance, style, and instrumentation: Use piano only, played simply and expressively with the left hand at an even pace and very *legato.* Tempo: moderately slow and tender, like a lullaby: quarter note = 76.

Teaching tips: In teaching the song, be simple yet expressive. It is in simplicity that one often finds the abundance of Christ's simple giving of himself.

Reference: See Regis J. Armstrong and Ignatius C. Brady, *Praying with St. Francis* (London: W. B. Eerdmans Publishing Co., 1987). *A Day in Your Presence, Rekindling the Inner Life: A 40-Day Journey in the Company of Francis of Assisi, arranged by David Hazard* (Minneapolis, MN: Bethany House Publishers, 1992).

90, Gloire à Dieu / Glory to God

Author/Composer: Claire-Lise Meissner-Schmidt, b. 1967, France

Background: This canon was presented by Claire-Lise Meissner-Schmidt, a United Methodist pastor from Strasbourg, France, at the annual meeting of the Global Praise Working Group at Hasliberg-Reuti, Switzerland, in 1998. The text is based on Luke 2:14.

Theme: The text is the song of the angels at the birth of Christ.

Liturgical use: Christmas Eve and Christmas Day. It is an excellent introit for Christmas Eve and Christmas Day worship services.

Performance and style: The canon should be sung by three groups of singers and should be sung *a cappella.* Tempo: quarter note = 100-108.

Teaching tips: Have the entire group or congregation sing the melody through once or twice before beginning the canon.

91/92, Sekim angelais visi / Let us join the angels' song

Author: Merkelis Šuoba, b. 1624, d. 1663, Lithuania

Composer: unknown, Lithuanian folk melody; trans., Per Harling, b. 1948, Sweden; harm., Carlton R. Young, b. 1926, USA

Background: In Lithuania, as in all the other Baltic countries, the churches had a hard time surviving during the years of the communist regime. What survived were the songs of the people, including the church's songs/hymns. People continued to sing their songs of hope and glory, revealing the power and the strength of music. People may be oppressed, jailed, or even killed, but their songs will never be imprisoned or destroyed. Songs survive.

   This is a Lithuanian, Lutheran hymn from the seventeenth century. There is a strong influence of Lutheran hymnody among the Protestant churches of the Baltic states. The folk melody has been well-known throughout Europe since medieval times.

Theme: In this hymn, we share the song of the angels at the birth of Christ, a *gloria,* which has been included in Eucharistic liturgies.

Liturgical use: This hymn may be used as the *Gloria/laudamus* in a traditional Protestant service, or as an Advent or Christmas hymn.

Performance, style, and instrumentation: The song could easily be learned by the choir singing the stanzas and the congregation singing the refrain. Then they may join together. The hymn may be sung with keyboard or organ accompaniment, though *a cappella* singing would be preferred. Tempo: quarter note = 90.

93, As on the cross the Savior hung

Author: Samuel Stennett, b. 1727, Exeter, Devonshire, Great Britain; d. 1795, Muswell Hill, Middlesex, Great Britain
Composer: Unknown; adapt. from *Sacred Harmony and Musical Companion* (1835) by Carlton R. Young, b. 1926, USA
Background: See John Rippon's *Baptist Selection,* 1787; Rippon, b. 1751 Tiverton, Devonshire, UK; d. 1836, London, UK. As a pastor and the editor of the *Baptist Annual Register,* 1790-1802. The text is based on the words of Jesus to the thief on the cross in Luke 23:43.

   The tune THE CONVERTED THIEF first appeared in William *Southern Harmony and Musical Companion,* 1835, where it is set in three parts for bass, melody, and upper voice.
Theme: The suffering of Christ
Liturgical use: Passion Sunday, Passion Week, Good Friday
Performance and style: In nineteenth-century US singing-school performance practice, the melody and upper voices are sung by both male and female voices, resulting in a unique and rich six-part texture. The melody may be effectively sung unaccompanied by solo or soli voices. Portions of the passion of Jesus Christ (for example, verses from Matthew 26-27) may be read preceding each stanza. Tempo: dotted half note = 60.

94, Este momento / This is the moment

Author/Composer: Pablo Sosa, b. 1933, Argentina; Eng. trans., S T Kimbrough, Jr., 1936, USA; arr., Jorge Lockward, b. 1965, Dominican Republic
Background: This song was written for the opening worship service of the 1990 school year at ISEDET (Instituto Superior Evangélico de Estudios Teológicos), the ecumenical theological seminary in Buenos Aires where the author was a teacher. Dr. Eugene Stockwell, who was at that time being installed as the new President of ISEDET, chose to preach on the same subject. The main idea of *Este momento* ("This time") was to analyze the present situation of the world (country, church, etc.) and reflect on what we, as Christians, can do about it. The

author of this song text felt that, if we were to be honest with ourselves, we would realize that we have nothing to offer to others except our trust in a God "who has not forgotten," and to stand together, seeking "to change their cry into a song."[4]

The words are written in a rather "classical," formal, poetical style. To balance this, Sosa chose to set them to a very popular kind of music, *candombe*, a musical form brought to the Río de la Plata area (Argentina and Uruguay) by Africans.

Theme: The composer bids us listen to three distinct voices: the despairing cry of people in need, God's voice revealed in Jesus Christ, and our own voices as we attempt to turn "the painful cry into a song."

Liturgical use: This is a song about commitment, mission, witnessing, evangelizing. It is appropriate for commissioning of missionaries and ordination.

Performance and style: The musical and vocal style should be strongly rhythmical, stressed, and dramatic. Articulate the words of the stanzas expressively, almost in a recitative style.

The rhythm is known as *candombe.* The basic candombe rhythm is as follows: first beat: dotted eighth, sixteenth, / tied to second beat: dotted eighth, sixteenth, / tied to third beat: eighth, / eighth and fourth beat: a quarter note. Variations are welcome.

Note the dynamics: stanzas *mf*, refrain *ff.*

The song is a vigorous dance. One is not asked to dance while singing, but with some adequate coaching some of the group could dance. Tempo: quarter note = c. 80

Instrumentation: Originally only drums were used, but in contemporary presentation one may use the piano, accordion, guitar. Brass instruments also sound very good, closer to jazz.

Teaching tips: Set the rhythm either by clapping or using the percussion instruments. Give people a chance to play the instruments. Teach the refrain first. Then sing the stanzas and have people join in the refrain. The next time, they can also try the stanzas.

Reference: Although *candombe* provides the expression of a very important popular culture movement (called *murga*) in Buenos Aires, Argentina, it is on the other side of the de la Plata river in Montevideo, Uruguay, that *candombe* has become a more sophisticated musical form, and well developed versions have been recorded. If available, the recordings of Ruben Rada or Jaime Ross are helpful.

Recorded on *Tenemos Esperanza* (CD 1-016, GBGMusik), and on

Éste es el Día: Canciones de Pablo Sosa, a product of ISEDET (Buenos Aires, Argentina).

95, Courage, my soul (The storm is passing over)

Author/Composer: Charles Albert Tindley, b. 1851, d. 1933

Background and theme: "Courage, my soul" is one of forty gospel hymns composed by Charles Albert Tindley (1851-1933), an African American Methodist clergyman and hymn writer. As in many of his hymns, the basic focus is valiancy and patience in the midst of trials and tribulations.

Theme: In this hymn, the faithful are asked to persevere because the storm will soon be over. The refrain reiterates the theme—"the storm is passing over, hallelujah." The most familiar version of this concept is his hymn "Stand by Me," in which he invokes the presence and power of God to bring persons through the raging "storms of life."

Liturgical use: It is quite appropriate for Lent and Passion Week in the Christian church year. It may also serve as an appropriate response to sermons and scriptures regarding suffering and courage.

Performance, style, and teaching tips: The teaching methodology will depend largely on the assembly. Some persons will recognize the traditional nineteenth-century styles adopted by Tindley and have no difficulty following the dotted rhythms and the aggressive momentum. Others may require longer teaching periods at a slower speed. The words and texts are well matched, and the refrain can become a memorable experience. Tempo: quarter note = ca. 66.

Instrumentation: Piano or organ

96, What wondrous love is this

Text/Music: Traditional early American folk hymn

Background: This anonymous folk hymn is a favorite of nineteenth-century, rural, shape-note singers. The words appeared as early as Stith Mead's *General Selection of the Newest and Most Admired Hymns and Spiritual Songs Now in Use* (1811, 2nd enlarged edition). The tune first appeared in the appendix of the 1840 (2nd) edition of William Walker's *Southern Harmony and Musical Companion* (1835). The structure of the text may have been borrowed from the English ballad "Captain Kidd."

Theme: God has shown wondrous love to all humankind in the gift of the divine Son, Jesus Christ, who gave his life for all.

Liturgical use: It is appropriate for Passion Week, Easter, and general use.

Performance and style: In nineteenth-century US singing-school performance practice, the melody and upper voice were sung by both male and female voices, resulting in a unique and rich six-part texture. In stanzas 2 and 3, this poignant Dorian melody may be effectively sung by solo voices, unaccompanied. Tempo: half note = ca. 66.

Reference: It is recorded on *Steal Away to Jesus* (CD 1-005, GBGMusik). A contemporary choral setting by John Darnell is available from GBGMusik's *GP Choral Series* and is included on the accompanying CD *Anthem Sampler.* A choral German-language choral arrangement is published by Verlag Singende Gemeinde (Wuppertal, Germany).

97, Kom i sorgen / Come, O God, into my sorrow

Author/Composer: Per Harling, b. 1948, Sweden; harm., Carlton R. Young, b. 1926, USA

Background: A former classmate of Pastor Per Harling had suddenly died, and he was asked by the widow to be in charge of the funeral, at which only the immediate family was to gather. Harling had also been asked to sing a solo at the funeral. He did not know what to sing, but the night before the funeral this song slowly emerged. It was sung *a cappella* in the small chapel as the family surrounded the coffin.

Theme: The song is an invitation to God, who bears all sorrow, to share the sorrow one is enduring at the moment.

Liturgical use: It is appropriate for funerals or special memorial services, especially at times of sudden death and sorrow.

Performance, style, and instrumentation: The song should be sung slowly with deep reflection and may be accompanied on an organ/piano or sung *a cappella.* Tempo: quarter note = 76.

98, Yo quiero ser / I want to be

Author/Composer: Unknown, Latin America

Background and theme: The text for this song was inspired by Jeremiah 18:1-6 and Isaiah 64:8, and expresses a total surrender to God's will and a desire for a new beginning.

Liturgical use: It may be used effectively as preparation and response to the reading of the Word, as a prayer of consecration for the offertory, or as a response to the call to Christian discipleship.

Performance, style, and instrumentation: This is a reflective song that should be sung at a tempo of quarter note = 80-88. Consider a quiet accompaniment by piano or guitar using arpeggiated chords or with the flute stops on the organ using legato chords.

Reference: It is recorded on *Faith•Hope•Love* (CD 1-013, GBGMusik) and on *Tenemos Esperanza* (CD 1-016, GBGMusik).

99, Come, ye sinners, poor and needy

Author/Composer: Joseph Hart, b. 1712, d. 1768, London, Great Britain; transcr. and arr., Carlton R. Young, b. 1926, USA

Background: The hymn was first published in the author's *Hymns Composed on Various Subjects*, 1759. The affinity of its key evangelical words and phrases to revivalist preaching and worship practice made it a mainstay of song leaders of Reconstruction-Era urban revivals, who apparently added the refrain "I will arise" from a popular ballad about the parable of the Prodigal Son. The tune and text first appeared in this form in Philip P. Bliss's *Gospel Songs* (1874).

Theme: Repentance and salvation

Liturgical use: Invitation hymn within or following the sermon

Performance and style: This transcription from *Southern Harmony and Musical Companion* (1835) may be sung using nineteenth-century singing-school performance practice, whereby the melody and upper voice are sung by both male and female voices, with strong accents on beats one and three. The refrain may be sung following the first and fourth stanzas. Stanzas may be sung unaccompanied by solo or soli voices, or in the form of a canon (at one measure). Tempo: quarter note = 110. *A cappella* singing is preferred.

100, Ae kau tau a e 'otua / Christians, join the cause of Jesus

Author/Composer: Unknown, Tonga; transcr., I-to Loh, b. 1936, Taiwan; trans. Ronald Hines, b. USA

Background: Hines is a United Methodist pastor in Seattle and former missionary and professor at Union Theological Seminary, Manila,

Philippines. The hymn has been recorded by a Tongan congregation in Melbourne, Australia.

Theme: Mission, spiritual warfare, hope

Liturgical use: It is appropriate as a response to the call for commitment and/or sending forth. Christian year: general use, Easter.

Performance and style: For singing style, see *GP2,* #60, "Me yaco mai" ("Your kingdom come"). In order to demonstrate the spirit of mission, the bass part should be sung with vigor and powerful chest voice. Tempo: quarter note = ca. 112. Sing *a cappella.* Singing in the original language can be more powerful than singing in English.

Teaching tips: Have the choir sing the three upper parts (with the tenor singing the middle voice or the alto part at the actual pitch level, and let the alto sing the third voice) so that the complete triads are all heard.

101, O mnus oeuy Preah bahn bong-hagn / For the Lord has shown to all of us

Author: Sarin Sam, b. 1941, Cambodia, based on Micah 6:8

Composer: Sarin Sam

Background: The author/composer was commissioned in 1999 by the General Board of Global Ministries of The United Methodist Church to compose this song. Its purpose is to plead with God's people to follow the divine will as God's redeemed children in this world. Then they will be able to show the world the nature of God through deeds of mercy and justice and a humble walk with God.

Theme: God has expectations of humankind. The prophet Micah articulates them clearly in this passage: love mercy and kindness, do justice, and walk humbly with God. Those who fulfill these divine expectations will express themselves in the same manner.

Liturgical use: It is appropriate for general use, Holy Communion, and Love Feasts.

Performance and style: The vocal style is unison singing. It could also be sung as a solo. This song should be sung slowly with soft and gentle dynamics. Tempo: half note = 65-70.

Instrumentation: Use piano, strings, flute; and percussion and bass, if desired.

Teaching tips: Playing an instrument, such as a violin or flute, would be helpful in learning the melody. The leader should pronounce the words clearly with the sound of the music so the people may adapt their voices accordingly.

102, The church is like a table

Author: Frederik Herman Kaan, b. 1929, the Netherlands
Composer: I-to Loh, b. 1936, Taiwan
Background: The music was composed during the six-hour transit at Johannesburg Airport, South Africa, 1997, on the way to Harare, Zimbabwe, for the preparation of worship services for the eighth General Assembly of the World Council of Churches, 1998. Having been involved in ecumenical worship services for nearly three decades, the composer felt the pain of not being able to sit at the Communion table with certain Christians. The table, which is a symbol of unity in Christ, is well depicted by Kaan as one without corners or first or last places. Such an all-embracing grace prompted the composer to use *mi fa la ti do mi* scale to communicate the kind of intimate feeling of sharing.
Theme: The song emphasizes unity in Christ through the Holy Communion, resulting in: justice and equality, healing and reconciliation, humility and service.
Liturgical use: It is an appropriate preparation for any service of Holy Communion. During the Christian year, it may be used on Maundy Thursday, on World Communion Sunday, and at Love Feasts.
Performance, style, and instrumentation: The figurations on the tenor part are imitations of the Indonesian plucked zither, the style of which is similar to that of the *gamelan.* Accompaniment with harpsichord or guitars would add an intimate feeling. Tempo: quarter note = ca. 84.
Teaching tips: Teach the scale, *mi fa la ti do mi,* ascending and descending. Sing softly with intimate feeling in unison.

103, Sound a mystic bamboo song

Author: William Livingstone (Bill) Wallace, b. 1933, New Zealand
Composer: I-to Loh, b. 1936, Taiwan
Background: The text captures the realities of Asian cities by depicting Christ in tribal clothes, living in a squatter's shed. This inspired I-to Loh to compose this song, utilizing tribal/folk melodies of the Kalinga, northern Philippines, and those of the Amis, eastern Taiwan. Both

"dong dong ay . . ." and "na-lo-an-a . . . ." are non-lexical syllables that acquire mood, feelings, or meanings from the text and melody sung before or after them. The reason for integrating two ethnic traditions here is that many Filipino manual laborers in Taiwan frequently compete with the labor forces of the local tribal people, creating tensions and animosity. Putting the two melodies together is a symbol of calling for mutual acceptance, respect, trust, and cooperation. They need each other. The counterpoint shows the beauty of living and working together in harmony!

Theme: There are many emphases: praise, Christlike living, working and suffering with Asian people, human dignity, bondage and freedom, sharing, prayers for wholeness, growth, and worth.

Liturgical use: The song has multiple uses—Christian year: general use, Easter, Advent, Labor Sunday, World Communion Sunday, Ecumenical Sunday, gathering for celebration, commitment to freedom and justice.

Performance and style: Dance in any style familiar or popular in any culture in which the song is sung. Tempo: quarter note = ca. 96.

Instrumentation: Use bamboo buzzers and/or bamboo tubes to link the beats.

Teaching tips: Sing according to the suggestions made at the bottom of the page in the *GP2* songbook.

104/105, Nye khram, nye zolotoye zdanye / The church of God is not a temple

Author: Ivan Stepanovitch Prokhanov, b. 1869, d. 1935, Russia; Eng. trans., S T Kimbrough, Jr., b. 1936, USA

Composer: Anonymous, Russian folk song

Background: It is believed that this hymn was written in the 1920s at the time of great religious persecution of all Christians under the communists in Russia. Prokhanov was one of the most outstanding Protestant hymn writers in Russian church history. Many of his hymns have been preserved in the hymnody of the Baptist Church in Russia. A leader of the Russian Evangelical Association, he published thirteen books of hymns and translated many hymn texts into Russian. He was a composer and authored of many of his own texts.

Theme: The text paints a vivid picture of the church of God as a family of the faithful willing to accept all into its fellowship. It transcends all buildings and is a body of believers from all corners of the globe who gather around the cross of Christ.

Liturgical use: It is appropriate for services of consecration and ordination, as an opening hymn, and after the sermon.

Performance and style: It is Russian folk music and may be sung *a cappella* by a choir or congregation. Piano or organ is optional. One might gradually build up the affirmation of the hymn text by beginning *piano* and growing to *mezzo forte* and *forte.* Tempo *lento:* quarter note = 80.

Teaching tips: Have the keyboard play the melody line through, then have it sung by the choir in unison (men and/or women). Thereafter invite the congregation to join in unison. Sing in parts only after the melody has been learned.

References: It is recorded on *Faith•Hope•Love* (CD 1-013, GBGMusik).

106, If we love one another

Author/Composer: I-to Loh, b. 1936, Taiwan

Background: Based on 1 John 4:12, this song was originally written in Taiwanese for the closing worship at a retreat of Tainan Theological College and Seminary. It was one of the first times that the composer tried to use the familiar and preferred Western musical style of the students, yet with certain distinct features of oriental melodies. Music in minor mode seems to convey more intimate feelings of love, caring, and sharing. The constantly moving figures in the accompaniment seem to depict the inner power of God motivating and urging people to love one another.

Theme: God's love and human love

Liturgical use: It may be used as a response to sermons on love, commitment, passing of the peace, reconciliation before or after Holy Communion. Christian year: general use, World Communion Sunday, marriage ceremony.

Performance and style: It may be sung antiphonally between the choir and the congregation, or between the congregation divided by age groups, sexes, or different interest groups. All join together to conclude the last phrase to symbolize the perfection of God's love. Tempo: quarter note = ca. 80. See also teaching tips below.

Instrumentation: Keyboard is natural for this song, or use any aerophone (flute or recorder) to double the melody or improvise a counter melody, and a cello or other stringed instrument for the accompaniment.

Teaching tips: Since most of the texts and musical phrases are repeated, it would be interesting to create dialogues and interactions between different groups.

107/108, Kende, si ta mi ruman? / Brothers! Sisters! who are they?

Author/Composer: Richard Simon, b. 1936, Curaçao; arr., Patrick Prescod, b. 1932, island of Saint Vincent; trans., Kathleen M. Richardson, Curaçao; Eng. para., S T Kimbrough, Jr., b. 1936, USA

Background: Richard Simon, a retired high school English teacher, was born in Curaçao, Netherlands Antilles, on November 11, 1936, to devout Roman Catholic parents who were musicians. He attended teacher's training college at the "Bossche Kweekschool" in the Netherlands, where he would take existing religious songs written in Papiamentu, but sung to international tunes, and rearrange them into Antillean rhythms.

After studying piano and guitar, he began to compose songs for children (songbook: *Kanta Kantika Kontentu*) and songs for divine worship ("Kantika di Misa," Catholic Church, meaning "Songs for Service" and entitled *Misa Alegre*). "Kende, si ta mi ruman?" is one of the opening songs of the mass. Simon's *Misa Alegre* was the first songbook with local Antillean rhythms in Curaçao. Other songs had been written in Papiamentu, but had not been set to local rhythms.

"Kende, si ta mi ruman?" was first presented in December 1966 by the choir, Grupo Misa Alegre, of which Simon is a member, in the Chapel at the Dr. Capriles Clinic, an institution for the mentally challenged. The hymn is based on Jesus' response to the suggestion that his family members were waiting outside to see him, raising the question about who his family is. See Matthew 12:48-50.

Theme: The song highlights the oneness of Christ's family.

Liturgical use: Services of Christian unity, World Day of Prayer

Performance, style, instrumentation: The song is perhaps best accom-Panied with banjo, guitar, bass guitar, trumpet, bass drum, congas, scraper (grater). Tempo: quarter note = 110.

Teaching tips: Make everyone aware that in Curaçao, the language Papiamento (or Papiamentu) in which the song is written, is but one of at least four languages spoken—Dutch, Spanish, English, and Papiamento. Learn the refrain in the original language so that it may be sung by all.

Reference: It is recorded on *Caribbean Praise* (CD 1-011, GBGMusik).

109, Vengan, vengan todos / Come now, everybody

Author/Composer: Lois Kroehler, b. 1927, USA/Cuba

Background: Kroehler, a Presbyterian missionary in the city of Cárdenas, Cuba, was instrumental in shaping a new generation of Cuban church musicians and liturgists. While in Cuba, she edited *Toda la Iglesia Canta,* an ecumenical hymnal that included many new hymns from Cuban writers and composers. As part of her ministry, she composed children's songs for use in Christian camping experiences. "Vengan todos" is one of these songs.

Theme: This song is a call to the people of God to gather and work together, based on the story of the rebuilding of the walls of Jerusalem during the time of Nehemiah. When sung as a canon, the idea of "building up" is musically depicted together with the reality that while everyone has something different to offer, together all can create harmony.

Liturgical use: It makes a wonderful call to worship.

Performance, style, and instrumentation: This canon should be sung at a steady tempo of quarter note = ca. 120. Make sure that the first note of each musical phrase is accented. It is normally sung *a cappella,* but a two-measure accompaniment pattern for guitar or piano may be improvised with the following chords: G Em / Am D7 /.

Teaching tips: Before attempting to sing it as a canon, make sure the congregation is secure with the melody. Assign persons or groups to lead each section of the canon.

110, Njo, njo, njo / Jump for joy

Text/Music: Traditional song from Malawi

Background and theme: This song was perhaps first used in churches within the Blantyre Synod of the Church of Central Africa Presbyterian (CCAP), in southern Malawi. It is not restricted to the Presbyterian Church, however, but is also sung in many other denominations throughout Malawi. It is a chorus, which generally means that the words of the song are not found in the hymnbook but are learned and passed along through oral tradition.

In the first printing of *Global Praise 2* the Swahili word "njoo," which means "come," is misspelled "njo." It is pronounced as one syllable. Intone the "n" and elide it with the sound of the proper name "Joe" = "njoe." The remainder of the text is in Chichewa, one of Malawi's national languages and primarily spoken in the central and southern regions of the country. The presence of the Swahili text suggests that this chorus actually made its way into Malawi from Tanzania or Kenya (where Swahili is widely spoken). Perhaps some Malawians first heard this chorus while traveling in Tanzania or Kenya, or perhaps some Kenyans or Tanzanians visited Malawi and taught it to some people there. Because the song is so widespread and has been passed along orally, it is impossible to know exactly how Malawians came to sing it. When a song catches the imagination of people, it spreads like wildfire, and most attempts to discover its origins are futile. Perhaps the chorus was translated into Chichewa by Malawian Christians because they liked singing it and wanted to make it meaningful to their own context. It is probable that the one-syllable Swahili word "Njoo" was retained because the rhythm of repeating this text three times fits nicely with the jumping dance movement that some perform when singing this chorus. The word "come" in Chichewa is "bwe-ra" or "bwe-ra-ni," both of which have too many syllables to bring out the nice rhythm of the first part of the song. It is most likely that Malawian Christians decided to keep "njo" but translated the rest of the song into Chichewa.

Liturgical use: Within CCAP churches, choruses are usually sung at informal gatherings such as Sunday School classes, evangelism campaigns, meetings of youth groups and women's groups, etc. Sometimes choruses are sung at designated times during specific worship services. In other denominations, however, choruses may be sung regularly during Sunday worship. So the context and denomination determine when the chorus is sung.

Performance and style: Implicit in the act of translating a chorus to relate to one's situation is the fact that people feel free to change the words or insert new words to speak to the specific context of those singing. Thus, there are many versions of this song in Malawi, linked together by the familiar "Njoo, njoo, njoo" at the beginning of the piece. While

130

it is not common in North American churches with European roots to take the liberty of changing the words of a song to fit one's particular situation, it is a practice quite familiar to Malawians and to other Africans as well. At one point in Malawi's history, political enthusiasts changed the words of the song to speak against the notion of multi-lateralism coming into the country. The "Njoo, njoo, njoo" was retained for this version as well.

Much music in Malawi (and in other parts of Africa) is sung in a call-and-response style. That is, the leader of the singing "calls" or lines out the first words of the song or chorus and everyone responds with a refrain (either repeating the words the leader has lined out—as in the case of "Njoo, njoo, njoo"—or singing another simple refrain).

Since this is a lively chorus, it should be sung at a good, energetic tempo to encourage the singers to move to the music.

Instrumentation: This chorus may be sung with hand-clapping accompaniment or with drums, shakers, rattles, and other percussion instruments. This song was originally intended to be sung *a cappella,* though some have begun to use piano and guitar, even in Malawi.

Teaching tips: The vowels in the Chichewa text are pronounced as follows: a = saw, e = sleigh, i = ski, o = snow, u = sue. The consonants are pronounced: ph = pot, ng' = song.

111/112, Det kan va en tant / It can be a girl

Author/Composer: Tomas Boström, b. 1953, Sweden

Background and theme: Over a number of years Tomas Boström has written many songs for children. Often their inspiration came from different countries, experiences, and biblical stories, but most of all encounters with people. This song is an example of Boström's most typical themes—in everyone we can see the nearness of God.

Liturgical use: In Sweden it is common practice that at a particular point in the worship, a time is dedicated to the children. This song would be excellent for the World Day of Prayer and global awareness of God's creation. It is an excellent song with which to give thanks for friendship and for the church to emphasize its openness to everyone.

Performance and style: In the refrain, after the second handclap, open your arms like a door and turn around to envision the hope of the whole world open to everyone. When you repeat, you can turn the other way. Tempo: quarter note = 128.

Instrumentation: Keyboard, guitar, bass, percussion

Teaching tips: Let the children lead the congregation in the singing, the handclaps, a dance, and/or movement. This will help all to see God in the nearest friend and to see the nearest friend in God.

113, Enviado soy de Dios / Sent out in Jesus' name

Author: Unknown, Cuba; Eng. trans., Jorge E. Maldonado, b. 1944, Ecuador

Composers: Unknown, Cuba; arr., Carmen Peña, b. 1940, USA

Theme: This song reminds us of our partnership with God to build a world where love and justice prevail.

Liturgical use: The primary liturgical use of this song is for the Sending Forth at the conclusion of worship. Try it as a recessional with the whole congregation facing outward as all affirm in song their commitment to be God's presence in the world.

Performance, style, and instrumentation: Sing accompanied by percussion or sing *a cappella* in unison. Tempo: half note = 88.

Teaching tips: Teach this song in a call-and-response pattern in three sections: the first 8 measures as a unit, then measures 9-16, and then measures 17-24.

References: It is recorded on *Tenemos Esperanza* (CD 1-016, GBGMusik) and on the CD *Sent by the Lord* (GIA Publications, Inc., 7404 So. Mason Ave., Chicago, IL 60638; tel. 1-800 442-1358).

114, Jesus Christ sets free to serve

Author/Composer: I-to Loh, b. 1936, Taiwan

Background: This song was written as the theme song for the Eighth General Assembly of the Christian Conference of Asia held in Seoul, Korea, 1985. The location of the assembly motivated the composer to write in one of the typical Korean rhythmic patterns: a twelve-beat cycle accompanied by the *changgo,* a double-headed drum in the shape of an hourglass.

Theme: Mission of Christ and the church, fullness of life, sharing in the universality of the church

Liturgical use: Commitment, offertory, sending forth; Christian year: general use, mission Sunday

Performance and style: Sing *a cappella,* except for drum accompaniment. Tempo: dotted quarter note = ca. 52

Instrumentation: A drum accompaniment is a must for this piece.

Teaching tips: Divide the congregation or choir into two groups: one sings and the other claps the rhythmic patterns as notated.

115, Nurtured by the Spirit

Author/Composer: Per Harling, b. 1948, Sweden

Background and theme: In the summer of 1998, hundreds of young people from all parts of the world came together to a Youth Mission Event in New Hampshire, sponsored by the Women's Division of the United Methodist General Board of Global Ministries. The theme was "We are the seeds." Per Harling was invited to be one of the music leaders during the event and was also asked to compose the theme song. This song was the result. It soon became very popular among the young delegates and was sung almost every time they all came together for worship or for evening entertainments.

Liturgical use: The song may be sung any time when mission perspectives are emphasized and/or as a song of sending forth at the end of worship. It is also appropriate for Pentecost.

Performance and style: The song may be sung as a canon. Tempo: quarter note = 96.

Instrumentation: Keyboard and rhythm instruments

Teaching tips: When teaching it for the first time, sing it through a couple of times. Then divide the people into two groups of singers with two song leaders. The first group starts at the beginning as the other group begins the second part of the song. Perform the song preferably in a rock style, with a strong beat. Tempo: quarter note = 96.

Reference: It is recorded on *Global Praise 2* (CD 1-012, GBGMusik).

116, Ye servants of God

Author: Charles Wesley, b. 1707, d. 1788, Great Britain

Composer: Swee Hong Lim, b. 1963, Singapore

Background: The musical setting was composed to celebrate the life and ministry of Alex Ling, the father-in-law of the composer.

The original hymn written by Charles Wesley does not have a refrain. The refrain is a feature added to the hymn in the spirit of celebration.

Theme: Evangelism and mission, but it may also be used as a hymn of praise at the opening of worship.

Liturgical use: It is appropriate for an Evangelism or Mission Sunday, for all All Saints' Day, and as a call to worship.

Performance, style, and teaching tips: The hymn is upbeat in nature and should be sung with high energy. The notated accompaniment is merely a guide; performers need to ensure that the accompaniment is energetic and strong. Improvisation and the use of additional instruments for accompaniment is encouraged. Tempo: half note = 60-66.

The hymn consists of two eight-measure phrases and a refrain. It is possible to have a soloist sing the stanzas while the congregation sings the refrain. Alternatively, a soloist could sing stanza one and the congregation could be invited to join in the subsequent stanzas.

Instrumentation: A keyboard (piano, synthesizer, or organ) may be used, augmented with other instruments, such as a worship band consisting of guitars, drums, and other instruments, e.g., trumpets.

Reference: The hymn is recorded on *Faith•Hope•Love* (CD 1-013, GBGMusik).

117/118, Hành trang tuổi trẻ / We've packed for the journey

Author/Composer: Hoang Duc, Peter Mau Nguyen, Vietnam

Background: Unknown

Theme: Like many biblical psalms, this song tells the worshipers that they may bring their hurts and wounds as an offering to God in worship. There they may ask for God's help in building a new world. They come humbly and with penitent spirits, bringing all that they are and hope to be as they journey to the house of the Lord. This prepares them to go forth with God's help to build a new world.

Liturgical use: This song is appropriate as a call to worship or a hymn at the beginning of worship, for services of repentance and healing, and during Lent.

Performance and style: Interestingly, the song is not written in a Vietnamese pentatonic scale. It should be sung with specific attention to the dynamic levels of the two parts of the song. Sing the stanzas of stanzas of the song at a *mezzo forte* level and move to *forte* each time

the refrain is sung. Sing the entire song in unison. Tempo: quarter
note = 100.

Instrumentation: Generally, a keyboard instrument is used for accompaniment.

Teaching tips: Introduce the melody with the keyboard, then have a solo
singer sing one stanza. If you have Vietnamese persons in your
congregation or community, invite them to sing a stanza or two in their
native language.

Reference: The hymn appears in the United Methodist Vietnamese
hymnal.

119, There are tables in our city

Author: S T Kimbrough, Jr., b. 1936, USA
Composer: Carlton R. Young, b. 1926, USA
Background: Having seen so many homeless and hungry people in his
travels, the author of this text began to ask himself whether following
Christ meant literally taking the heavily laden table of food from
one's own home into the street for those without food, clothing, or
shelter. He came to the conviction that indeed Christ expects this of his
followers. The author wrote this text with the hope of providing a
means of celebrating this vital dimension of Christian living. The
jazz/blues style is used by the composer because it is typical of the
musical languages of the street in some parts of the world. The text
and setting were introduced at the Global Praise Working Group
meeting at Hasliberg-Reuti, Switzerland, in 1998.

Theme: Stewardship of resources is at the center of Christian living.
One cannot bypass this obligation or those who lack the basic needs
of life. When we commit ourselves to follow Christ, we commit to
share what we have with the needy.

Liturgical use: This song is appropriate for Stewardship Sunday, Advent,
or any season of the Christian year.

Performance and style: The song is best played in a jazz/blues style. A
solo singer may sing stanzas 1 and 2, with the congregation joining on
the remaining stanzas. The congregation will usually sing well if the
style is set by a soloist. However, do not sacrifice the message of the
song to the style. The singing should be relaxed, stressing the message.
"Scat" singing, however, is not intended, and elaborate embellishments are not appropriate. Tempo: quarter note = ca. 78.

Instrumentation: Keyboard is necessary. Guitar, bass guitar, and drum set (brushes only) may be added.

Teaching tips: Have the keyboard play a stanza first, emphasizing the melodic line. Afterward, have a solo singer, preferably someone who understands jazz/blues styles, sing one stanza for the congregation.

Reference: It is recorded on *Faith•Hope•Love* (CD 1-013, GBGMusik).

120/121/122, Ttugoun Maum / With passion in our hearts

Author: Ik Hwan Moon, b.1918, d. 1994, Korea

Composer: Don Hwan Cho, b. 1935, Korea; alt. Francisco F. Feliciano, b. 1941, Philippines

Background: Korean vocal music generally consists of a single melodic line. However, with western influence, part-singing has now become a part of Korean vocal tradition. According to I-to Loh, this particular song exhibits some semblance of traditional Korean music with its triple meter (3/4). In traditional court music, compound duple (6/8) meter predominates.

Francisco F. Feliciano is a well-known composer in the Philippines. He is also the founding president of the *Sambalikahaan*, an umbrella organization that seeks to strengthen the development of indigenous Christian liturgy and music in Asia through research and publication, education, and artist-in-residence programs. The Asian Institute for Liturgy and Music is the educational wing of this organization. This degree-granting institution offers training in both Asian and Western musical traditions. The *Sambalikahaan* itself is a retreat center that hosts a research and publication department, as well as residential and liturgical spaces for the development of indigenous liturgical expression.

Theme: Justice

Liturgical use: World Day of Prayer, services of healing

Performance and style: Korean vocal style tends to be strong. In this song, that should be observed. Part singing is encouraged, and the hymn is notated accordingly. Maintain a steady rhythm throughout to a drum beat. Tempo: quarter note = 92.

Teaching tips:

A Korean Christian could be invited to share about the life and history of the Korean church. At the same time, the person could speak briefly about the pain of separation between North and South

Korea and its impact on Korean families. Thereafter, the congregation could be invited to "hum" the melody, as a prayer for unity is uttered in Korean by the guest speaker. Thereafter the hymn may be sung by the choir in their vocal parts. Subsequently, stanzas may be sung by the congregation vocally supported by the choir.

Instrumentation: Flat hand drums

Reference: It is recorded on *Youth Mission Chorale: Asia Tour 2001* (CD 1-020, GBGMusik). A simple choral arrangement of this work is available from GBGMusik in the *GP Choral Series* (CS 1017) and is included on the accompanying CD, *Anthem Sampler.*

123/124, Min himmel / My heaven

Author/Composer: Per Harling, b. 1948, Sweden

Background and theme: The former Lutheran bishop of Sweden, Martin Lönnebo, a somewhat different mystic of modern times and much loved in broad circles, within and without the church, had many faith visions for his very secular diocese. (His tenure as bishop was before the separation of church and state in Sweden.) His coworkers at the diocesan office often grew tired of his sometimes-wild ideas. So when he told them that he wanted to advertise in the newspapers asking children in the diocese to write to him, telling him about their ideas/ visions of what heaven might be like, they nodded their heads, thinking: "Here we go again. . . . He will not get even *one* letter." But the bishop advertised and received thousands of letters! Sometime thereafter, he telephoned Per Harling, asking him if he could create a musical out of the children's letters, focusing not only on the heavenly visions of the children but also on environmental issues. The result was Harling's musical, *Fly, Pretty Angels, Fly!* "Min himmel," the opening song in the musical, includes a number of quotations from the children's letters.

Liturgical use: The song is appropriate for Thanksgiving and Harvest Festivals. The complete musical from which it comes is only twenty to twenty-five minutes in length and may be used in most worship services, especially where children take an active part. It has two possible endings: one which leads into the service of Holy Communion and one which does not.

Performance and style: If possible, invite someone who speaks Swedish to sing the song (or at least the first stanza) in Swedish. The last four bars may be played between the stanzas as an interlude. Tempo: dotted half note = 60.

Instrumentation: Keyboard, guitar, bass

Reference: It is recorded on *Fly, Pretty Angels, Fly!* (CD 1- 019, GBGMusik; piano/vocal book, and singer's edition [ISBN 1-890 569-41-0]). There is also a German-language version available (Edition Anker, Stuttgart, Germany).

125, Praise ye the Lord

Text: Psalm 150

Composer and textual adaptation: Judge Jefferson Cleveland, b. 1937, d. 1986, USA

Background: This black gospel setting of Psalm 150 is the direct response by the composer to an assignment during a gathering at Candler School of Theology, Emory University, in 1982, of musicians who were involved in the development of a number of denominational hymnals. The assignment given by the conference coordinator, Carlton R. Young, strongly encouraged each participant to compose a setting of a psalm in her or his own cultural or racial ethnic tradition. Judge Jefferson Cleveland responded the next day with this setting of Psalm 150, which was an immediate success and the only one presented that reflected the African American black gospel genre.

Judge Jefferson Cleveland served as professor of music at Claflin College, Langston University (Oklahoma City), Jarvis Christian College (Boston), and Wesley Theological Seminary (Washington, DC) and was also co-editor, with Verolga Nix, of the *Songs of Zion, Supplementary Hymnal,* published by The United Methodist Church in 1982. Cleveland contributed numerous arrangements of songs and hymns to various publications.

Theme: Praise of God the Creator and of all creation

Liturgical use: It may be used as the lectionary or appointed Psalm for the Day, and in services of praise and thanksgiving.

Instrumentation: Piano, organ, percussion

Performance, style, and teaching tips: The refrain may be taught by rote, even if there are music readers in the assembly. If there are sight-readers, they may serve as cantors for the stanzas, or one cantor may sing the stanzas until the melody is familiar. The entire song should be sung with enthusiasm and with as much vigor as possible. Tempo:

quarter note = 120.

126, Teka nzilo / Take fire

Author/Composer: Unknown, Mozambique
Background: This Xitswa rally song from Mozambique was transcribed
and harmonized by Carlton R. Young from the version sung by
William F. Anderson, former missionary to Mozambique, at the
Global Praise celebration of Belmont United Methodist Church,
Nashville, Tennessee, June 1999.
Theme: Empowerment in the life of the Spirit, Pentecost Sunday
Liturgical use: Opening of worship, gathering song
Performance and style: This gathering song should be sung vigorously in
a call-and-response style without pause between stanzas. Handclap-
ping and drums may be added. Soloists may sing the verses, and the
group sings the refrain in either the English phonetic syllabification
found below or the translated text. Tempo: quarter note = 88.
 The Latin characters representing the approximate sounds of the
Xitswa language in English phonetic syllabification are as follows:
>Oo yah hoo-mey-sah vah-nah-nah,
>Vah-nah vah Ah-free-kah;
>Oo yah hoo-mey-sah vah-nah-nah,
>Vah-nah vah Ah-free-kah.
Instrumentation: drums, *hosho* and other percussioin

127, Nada te turbe / Nothing can trouble

Author: Teresa de Avila, 16th century, Spain
Composer: Jacques Berthier, b. 1923, d. 1994, France
Background: The text for this song comes from a poem by the sixteenth-
century Spanish mystic Teresa de Avila, one of only three women to
be declared "doctors of the church" by the Roman Catholic Church.
The music is from French composer Jacques Berthier, who, until his
death in 1994, regularly collaborated with the Taizé community. Taizé
is a small village in the Burgundy region of France where an ecumenical community of religious brothers was founded in 1949 with the
purpose of becoming a "parable of communion," a place where people
seek to be reconciled every day. Faced with thousands of young people
who were making the pilgrimage to Taizé every year, the brothers

created chants for use with the young people. Little by little, over a period of nearly twenty years, a vast repertoire of original and altogether new music was created and became known throughout the world as the "Music from Taizé."

Theme: This is a song of deep trust in God.

Liturgical use: The music from Taizé is primarily music for prayer. This particular chant is very useful for prayers of intercession.

Performance, style, and instrumentation: Taizé chants are meant to be repeated again and again in a meditative manner, as a way of deepening one's understanding of the simple yet profound truths they proclaim. Consider starting the instrumentation with a single harmonic instrument such as piano, guitar, or organ and carefully adding other instruments and vocal descants upon repetitions of the song (for other instrumental and vocal parts, see resources below). This particular chant should be sung in a soft, subdued manner at a tempo of quarter note = ca. 66-72.

Teaching tips: Since Taizé chants are usually sung without direction, consider teaching the chant to a small choral group who would then serve as starters and leaders of the song. Be careful with the opening syncopations in measures 1, 2, and 4, which should be sung unaccented. There should be no breath between measures 3 and 4.

Reference: A recording and instrumental/vocal parts for this song are available: *Cantos de Taizé* (in Spanish), *Songs and Prayers from Taizé* (in English); GIA Publications, Inc., (7404 So. Mason Ave., Chicago, IL 60638; tel. 1-800 442-1358).

Endnotes

[1] Personal letter, August 8, 2004.

[2] Personal letter, August 8, 2004.

[3] Personal communiqué, June 2, 2004.

[4] Jorge Lockward, "Performance Notes" for songbook, *Tenemos Esperanza* (New York: GBGMusik, 2002).

Abbreviations

EM (2002)	=	*Mir Vam* (Peace be with you), hymnal of the Russia United Methodist Church (Moscow, 2002)
GP1	=	*Global Praise 1* songbook (New York: GBGMusik, 1996, rev. 1997, 1999, 2000)
GP2	=	*Global Praise 2* songbook (New York: GBGMusik, 2000)
VM (2002)	=	*Gesangbuch der Evangelisch-methodistischen Kirche* (Stuttgart, 2002), hymnal of The United Methodist Church in Germany, Austria, and Switzerland

GLOSSARY OF TERMS

a cappella
Without instrumental accompaniment. The original Italian term means literally "in the style of the chapel."

agogô, *GP2 #72*
Two- or three-cylindered Brazilian bell played with a round wooden mallet. The *agogô* bells are used in the *samba,* adding high-pitched sounds to the musical texture.

Examples of *agogô* patterns:

angklung, *GP2 #13*
Tuned bamboo slide rattles, native to Indonesia and also used in Malaysia and Thailand. Generally, they are made of two or three vertical bamboo tubes (tuned in octaves) attached to a handheld, horizontal bamboo rod. Slots in each tube align with a crosspiece that strikes the tube when the instrument is shaken.

baguala, *GP1 #61*
An intense, folkloric musical style with pre-Columbian roots from northern Argentina and southern Bolivia. Melodically, the *baguala* centers around the three pitches sung in a forceful, deliberate manner. It may be described as a "cry of the soul."

143

baião, *GP1 #2, GP2 #47/48*

A musical style from the Brazilian northeast. *Baião* melodies and harmonies are based on a dominant 7th chord. Rhythmically, *baião's* syncopated 2-4 pattern is defined by the *zabumba* drum.

Baião percussion patterns:

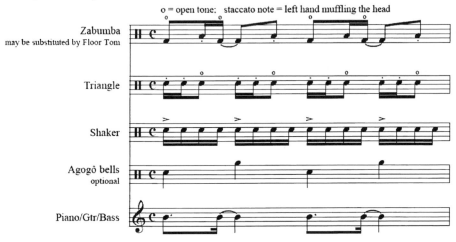

bandoneón, *GP2 #73*

A particular type of accordion invented in Germany by Heinrich Band in 1854 as an inexpensive substitute for church organs. By the end of the century, the *bandoneón* reached South America, where it was used as the preferred accompaniment for the *tango*. The sound of the *bandoneón* is sweeter than that of the accordion and its structure does not involve a keyboard but rather 33 buttons on the left and 38 on the right, each making a different sound in the expansion and contraction of the bellows.

bolero, *GP1 #15*

A romantic, rhythmical ballad of Cuban origin. The Cuban *bolero* combined elements of the Spanish 3/4 *bolero* and the English country dance with African percussive elements, resulting in a change from triple to duple meter (2/4 or 4/4). The instrumentation for the *bolero* usually includes guitar, conga or bongos, clave, and light maracas.

bombo legüero, *GP2 #28*

Large, cylindrical-shaped drum from the Andean region used in popular musical styles of Argentina, Chile, Bolivia, and Peru. The body of the drum is made out of a hollow tree, with mounted skins retaining the animal's fur, thus producing a very distinctive mellow and deep tone. The *bombo* is played with a stick and a mallet that strike the wooden rims and the head. A floor tom provides an alternative instrument, if a *bombo* is not available. Play the rim or the side of the tom with a stick in the right hand and the skin of the tom with a mallet in the left hand.

bossa nova, GP2 #52
A Brazilian musical style, which originated in Rio de Janeiro in the late 1950's, combining the rhythms of *samba* with the recitative melodies and rich harmonies of "cool" jazz. The *bossa nova* is often accompanied with guitar, piano, bass, and drum set (with brushes). Syncopation is predominant in the rhythmic patterns of the guitar, piano, and bass, while the drums maintain a pattern that emphasizes upbeats.

Bossa nova rhythmic pattern:

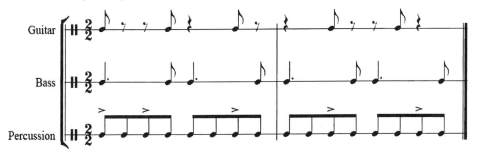

Byzantine Chant, *GP2 #55*
A monophonic (single melodic line) liturgical chant of the Greek Orthodox Church dating from the Byzantine Empire (330-1453). Although the *Phos Hilaron* (Gladdening Light) predates Byzantium, it is called "Byzantine" because of its use in the Byzantine Vespers liturgy.

calypso, GP1 #24, #60
A Caribbean musical style, which originated in the island of Trinidad. Originally, the lyrics of a calypso were impromptu, humorous rhymes created by a singer in the midst of a contest.

Calypso conga pattern:

O = open tone   S = slap

candombe, GP2 #94

A highly percussive African rhythm that came to the Río de la Plata area of South America. Presently found in Uruguay and Argentina, *candombe* is played in a drum corps using three different size drums, the *piano*, the *chico*, and the *repique*. For substitutes, try using a large conga drum tuned down low for the *piano*, a conga drum in normal tuning range for the *repique*, and a small *quinto* drum for the *chico*.

Candombe percussion patterns:

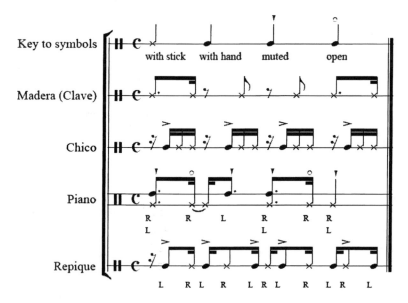

carnavalito, GP1 #28

A pre-Columbian, Andean rhythm found in Peru, Bolivia, and Argentina. The *carnavalito* is usually accompanied by the *charango*, a small double five-string guitar with a resonator box often made of the shell or skeleton of an armadillo. Other instruments used are the *zampoña*, an Andean pan flute; the *quena*, an Andean recorder flute; the *bombo legüero* (see above) and the *chakchas*, Andean shakers made out of goat hooves.

Carnavalito rhythmic pattern:

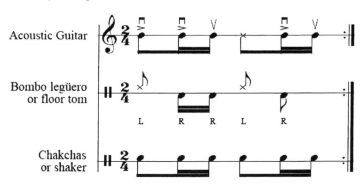

chamarrita, *GP1 #41*
A musical style from northern Argentina. Originally a popular dance of the Azores Islands, the *chamarrita* came to southern Brazil with Portuguese immigrants and from there made its way to eastern Uruguay and northern Argentina.

conga, *GP1 #8, #11, #24, #31, GP2 #108*
Single head, hollow Cuban drum derived from the Congolese *makuta* drums. It is also called *tumbadora*.

credo, *GP1 #35, GP2 #22*
The Latin word *credo* (I believe), indicates a summation of the principal articles of faith professed by the church. The *credo* is the third part of the "Ordinary" (unchanging) parts of the Roman Catholic Mass that are often set to music.

cueca, *GP1 #27*
Originally a Peruvian colonial dance, the *cueca* reached Chile and Argentina in the 1820s. Today it is considered the national dance of Chile.

Cueca guitar patterns:

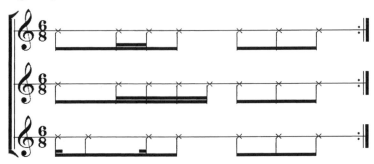

de profundis, *GP2 #18*
The Latin words *de produndis* are translated "out of the depths," and are the opening words of Psalm 30.

fermata (⌢), *GP1 #54, GP2 #20*
A musical symbol that indicates the prolongation of a tone beyond its expected value.

gamelan, *GP1 #17, GP2 #102*
Indonesian orchestra made of sets of tuned bronze (or iron/wood/bamboo) gongs, gong-chimes, metallophones, drums, flute, bowed and plucked strings, and sometimes singers. The gamelan requires concentrated group effort and a keen sense of rhythm as different instruments and musicians play the notes of the melody line in interlocking fashion.

gloria in excelsis, *GP2 #10*
The Latin *gloria in excelsis* means "glory in the highest." These are the beginning words of the angel's song in Luke 2:14. The *gloria* is the second part of the "Ordinary" (unchanging) parts of the Roman Catholic Mass that are often set to music.

glissandi, *GP2 #82*
The plural form of the Italian musical term *glissando,* which indicates sliding from one pitch to another.

Gregorian chant, *GP2 #55*
The plain chant repertory from the Roman Catholic Church. The final establishment of this repertory is generally assigned to the work of Pope

Gregory the Great (590-604). In colloquial use, Gregorian chant is used as a synonym for plainchant, a monodic (single melody) church music style of the early Middle Ages.

hemiola, *GP1 #27*
The rhythmical disruption of a triple meter by a duple figure or vice versa.

kyrie eleison, *GP1 #42, GP2 #17, #19, #68*
The Greek *kyrie eleison* (Lord, have mercy), often referred to as the *kyrie*, is an ancient Christian prayer. It is the first part of the "Ordinary" (unchanging) parts of the Roman Mass that are often set to music.

lundu, *GP2 #33*
An Afro-Brazilian dance and musical style brought to Brazil by Bantu slaves from Angola, the *lundu* was very popular in seventeenth- and early eighteenth-century Brazil.

modinha, *GP1 #65*
The *modinha*, a diminutive of *moda* (mode or style), is a Brazilian dance, which is directly derived from the Portuguese songs and dances of that name. Present day *modinhas* are sentimental in mood and similar to the Cuban boleros.

obbligato, *GP2 #45*
An additional instrumental or vocal melodic line.

ostinato, *GP2 #18*
The Italian word *ostinato* (stubborn), indicates a musical pattern that is repeated continuously.

pentatonic scale, *GP2 #28*
Musical scales composed of five notes, which form the basis of many folkloric styles.
Two common pentatonic scales:

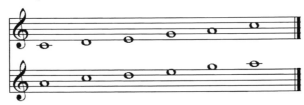

149

pífano, *GP2 #47/48*
A small, high pitched flute used in Spanish military bands.

portamento, *GP2 #18*
This Italian noun is derived from the verb *portare* (to carry) and designates a vocal or instrumental glide from one tone to another, without particular attention to the intervening tones.

raga, *GP1 #50*
A particular mode in Indian music, a *raga* may indicate at the same time the following: scale, modal structure, melodic direction, mood, movement and even time of day.

samba, *GP2 #72*
An Afro-Brazilian dance and musical style, *samba* is associated with the celebration of the *carnaval,* in which *samba* schools play, sing, and dance new compositions related to the yearly theme of the *carnaval.*

Samba pattern adapted to guitar, bass, and conga:

samba-canção, *GP1 #15*
A slower samba with a more elaborate vocal melody.

sanctus, *GP1 #33, #49, GP2 #21, #23, #24*
The Latin word *sanctus* means "holy" and designates an ancient Jewish prayer based on the hymn of the cherubim in Isaiah 6:3. It is the fourth part of the "Ordinary" (unchanging) parts of the Roman Catholic Mass that are often set to music.

sanctus* and *benedictus, *GP1 #33*
The Latin words *sanctus* (holy) and *benedictus* (blessed), refer to a

Christian combination of the hymn of the *cherubim* in Isaiah 6:3 and the quotation of Psalm 118:25-26 used in Jesus' triumphal entry into Jerusalem (Matthew 21:9). The *sanctus* and *benedictus* are the fourth and fifth parts of the "Ordinary" (unchanging) parts of the Roman Catholic Mass that are often set to music.

tabla, *GP1* #8
A pair of single-headed Indian drums. The higher pitched drum (*dayan*) is played with the right hand and the larger one (*bayan*) with the left. The *dayan* is tuned to the fundamental note in the scale or occasionally to the 5th above. The *bayan* is tuned to the fundamental or fifth above, an octave lower than the *dayan*.

tamborito, *GP2* #41
A Panamanian dance and musical style with African roots.

tango, *GP1* #25, #59, *GP2* #73
A dance and musical style from the Río de la Plata region of Argentina and Uruguay, the *tango* originated in the bars, cafes, and houses of ill repute of Buenos Aires in the 1880's. At first, it was considered socially unacceptable, but eventually became an integral part of Argentinean and Uruguayan cultures.

zabumba, *GP2* #47/48
A large bass drum from northern Brazil.

Index of Authors, Composers, Translators, Arrangers,

(Names are followed by selection numbers from *GP1* and *GP2*.)

Feliciano, Francisco F., *GP2:* 121, 122
Forget, Daniel H., *GP2:* 127

Garbuzova, Julia, *GP2:* 25, 26
Garbuzova, Ludmila, *GP1:* 5, 62; *GP2:* 25, 26, 68, 69, 70
Gouël, Joëlle, *GP1:* 27, 49
Gray, Dorothy, *GP1:* 19
Green, Fred Pratt, *GP1:* 57
Gutierrez-Achón, Raquel, *GP1:* 40(a-1)

Handt, Hartmut, *GP1:* 26, 27, 49; *GP2:* 42
Harling, Per, *GP1:* 25, 34, 35, 44; *GP2:* 21, 34, 44, 54, 58, 91, 92, 97, 115, 123, 124
Hart, Joseph, *GP2:* 99
Henderson, Clara, *GP2:* 110
Hesla, Bret, *GP2:* 36
Hines, Ronald, *GP2:* 100
Ho Lung, Richard, *GP2:* 3
Hofstra, Marilyn, *GP1:* 19, 32
Hudson, Ralph E., *GP2:* 11

Ik, Hwan Moon, *GP2:* 120, 121, 122

Jackson, Mary K., *GP1:* 63; *GP2:* 17, 88
Jaén, Néstor, *GP2:* 41
Janssens, Peter, *GP1:* 10
Jawati, Max, *GP1:* 46
Jean-Pierre, Fede, *GP1:* 11, 13, 14
Jones, Ivor H., *GP1:* 57(a)
Jordan, Paschal, *GP2:* 56

Kaan, Fred, *GP1:* 39; *GP2:* 102
Kala, Ernest, *GP2:* 71
Kamadjadja, Jusuf, GP2: 45
Kauka, Dean T., *GP2:* 30, 71, 74
Kauwalu, Samuel, *GP2:* 71
Kimbrough, S T, Jr., *GP1:* 10, 11m 13, 14, 21, 22, 23, 26, 30, 33, 37, 55, 56, 62, 63, 67; *GP2:* 4, 5, 9, 23, 29, 30, 40, 41, 42, 43, 45, 49, 52, 57,

59, 63, 64, 67, 68, 70, 71, 74, 78, 83, 87, 90, 94, 98, 101, 105, 108, 117, 119, 122
Kimbrough, Timothy E., *GP1:* 37, 54, 55; *GP2:* 10, 22, 43, 45, 46
Knotts, Alice G., *GP1:* 26
Kroehler, Lois, *GP2:* 109
Kudirka, Darius, *GP2:* 64
Kuptarat, Solo, *GP2:* 51

Lagi, Rudolf, *GP2:* 44
Lee, Geonyong, *GP1:* 16
Lin, Shengben, *GP1:* 20
Lim, Swee Hong, *GP1:* 58; *GP2:* 61, 63, 84, 85, 116
Ling, Maria Poh Choo, *GP2:* 61
Lockward, Jorge A., *GP1:* 41, 59; *GP2:* 20, 94
Lockwood, George, *GP1:* 40(a-2)
Loh, I-to, *GP1:* 17; *GP2:* 6, 32, 50, 51, 60, 79, 100, 102, 103, 106, 114
Loperena, William, *GP2:* 24
Lubis, T., *GP2:* 13
Luíz, Gelson, *GP2*: 73
Lukashin, Andrei, *GP1*: 62

MacArthur, Terry, *GP2*: 75
Maka, Jacob, *GP2*: 30, 74
Maldonado, Jorge E., *GP2:* 113
Mam, Barnabas, *GP2:* 1
Markay, Kristen, *GP2:* 64
Maraschin, Jaci, *GP1:* 15
Matsikenyiri, Patrick, *GP1:* 36, 45; *GP2:* 5, 8, 83
McClellan, Doreen, *GP2:* 82
McGuckin, John A., *GP2:* 55
McLane, George, *GP2*: 71
Meissner-Schmidt, Claire-Lise, *GP2:* 90
Mesnyankina, Zoya, *GP2:* 68
Miagkova, Irina, *GP2*: 67
Minchin, James, *GP2:* 32
Molefe, S. C., *GP1:* 4
Monteiro, Simei, *GP1:* 2, 15, 65; *GP2:* 18, 33, 47, 48, 72
Moore, William, *GP2:* 93
Mozart, Wolfgang A., *GP1:* 3

Mulrain, George, *GP1:* 24, 31; *GP2:* 31, 37
Murray, John, *GP2:* 29
Murray, Shirley Erena, *GP1:* 17, 34, 40, 66; *GP2:* 34, 35
Mxadana, George, *GP1:* 4

Nhlane, Ben, *GP1:* 46
Nguyen, Peter Mau, *GP2:* 117, 118

Obleschuk, Walter G., *GP2:* 76
Owaldas, Honoratas, *GP2:* 64

Pagura, Frederico, *GP1:* 59
Pangaribuan, Dewi, *GP2:* 13
Peña, Carmen, *GP2:* 113
Perera, Homero R., *GP1:* 59
Pharris, Bill Dexheimer, *GP2:* 36
Phu, Xuan Ho, *GP2:* 118
Plüss, David, *GP2:* 42
Puloka, T. M., *GP1:* 21, 22
Pope, Marion, *GP1:* 16
Prescod, Patrick E., *GP1:* 60; *GP2:* 3, 107, 108
Price, Frank W., *GP2:* 80
Prokhanov, Ivan Stepanovitch, *GP2:* 104, 105

Richardson, Kathleen, *GP2:* 108
Rippon, John, *GP2:* 93
Runeberg, Johan L., *GP2:* 44
Ruppel, Paul Ernst, *GP1:* 26

Saint Francis of Assisi, *GP2:* 89
Sam, Sarin, *GP2:* 1, 23, 101
Schwarz, Joachim, *GP1:* 6
Sigurbjörnsson, T., *GP2:* 54
Simon, Richard, *GP2:* 107, 108
Sing, Mary, *GP2:* 71
Sosa, Pablo, *GP1:* 27, 41, 61; *GP2:* 28, 82, 94
Stainer, John, *GP1:* 29
Stennett, Samuel, *GP2:* 93
Sullivan, Leona, *GP1:* 32

Suoba, Merkelis, *GP2:* 91, 92
Suri, Ellison, *GP2:* 19
Sutton, Joan, *GP2:* 33

Tallis, Thomas, *GP2:* 39
Taylor, Karen, *GP2:* 27
Teresa of Ávila, *GP2:* 127
Thangaraj, Thomas, *GP1:* 8, 50
Tindley, Charles A., *GP2:* 95
Tinio, Rolando, *GP2:* 13
Trautwein, Dieter, *GP1:* 4, 39, 64
Tupouniua, Alipate, *GP1:* 21
Tuwere, I. S., *GP2:* 60

Uqueio, Zacharias M., *GP2:* 4

Walker, William, *GP2:* 96
Wallace, Bill, *GP2:* 103
Wang, Weifan, *GP1:* 20
Wesley, Charles, *GP1:* 7, 52, 53, 54, 63; *GP2:* 11, 39, 81, 84, 85, 116
Wesley, Samuel Sebastian, *GP1:* 53
Whalum Wendell, *GP1:* 58
White, Evelyn D., *GP2:* 86
White, Michael, *GP2:* 31
Wiant, Bliss, *GP2:* 80
Wren, Brian, *GP1:* 9

Yang, Sou, *GP2:* 77, 78
Yang, Zong Her, *GP2:* 77, 78
Young, Carlton R., *GP1:* 5, 7, 9, 11, 13, 21, 22, 25, 31, 34, 35, 40, 42, 49, 60, 62, 66, 67; *GP2:* 34, 35, 44, 53, 55, 81, 87, 91, 92, 93, 97, 99, 111, 112, 117, 119, 120

Index of First Lines / Global Praise 1

First lines are followed by selection numbers. Titles are in parentheses.
(a) indicates the Appendix of the songbook.

Index of First Lines / Global Praise 2

The first lines are followed by selection numbers. Titles and scripture references are in parentheses.